DRUG ABUSE AND YOUTH

DRUG ABUSE AND YOUTH :
A PSYCHOLOGICAL STUDY

A. K. Sen
Anis Ahmed

GYAN PUBLISHING HOUSE
NEW DELHI - 110002

DRUG ABUSE AND YOUTH

(Pharmacy, Chemistry, Health, Law)

ISBN : 81-212-0636-7

Published in 1999 in India by
Gyan Publishing House
5, Ansari Road
New Delhi 110 002
Laser Typesetting : Grow Computers, Delhi.
Printed at Mehra Offset Press. New Delhi.

To

Fond memory of Prof. (Mrs.) Anima Sen who was a distinguished Professor of Delhi University, and a person with moral courage, love and humanity.

PROFESSOR ANIMA SEN
(1938-1995)

CONTENTS

FOREWORD

The intensified need for going into the depth of drug abuse has attracted the social workers, behavioural scientists and the government machinery. The problem of alcoholism and drug addiction has become so serious that steps are to be taken for preventing serious maladjustment. The prevention is essential not only for the individual but for the society at large. The present generation, particularly the youth population, is passing through a critical stage which is characterized by crisis of identity, tension, violence and defiance. The unfortunate trend is that people presume that students are turning more and more towards alcoholism and drug addiction just to minimize their tension, anxiety and frustration. This acceptance of the fact has blocked the more comprehensive approach towards the understanding of the problem associated with drug abuse. Researches are needed in a highly scientific way to study the relative importance of biological, psychological and socio-cultural influence on the drug-taking behaviour. It is our general observation that drug abuse is more prevalent among the students, factory workers and also the persons belonging to high socio-economic group. The students are becoming addicted because of various reasons associated with undefined educational goal, lack of employment opportunities, unhealthy socio-political set-up, exploitation and economic crisis, etc. Such situations are further aggravated by the blind acceptance of western culture, lack of moral or religious education, unhealthy supervision and guidance, polluted university and school environment, lack of desirable models of learning, unhealthy effect of mass media and a need for identification with a specific group. The fashion of being drug abused has been highly accelerated by the movies depicting the heroic character indulging in wine, women and violence. The immature youth population become victim of all such depictions and adopt the behaviour of heroic character just for the purpose of identification. However, the explanation of drug addiction in terms of imitating behaviour, polluted environment and craze for western fashion cannot be sufficient in itself because there are multiple factors which contribute towards drug-taking behaviour. The joint contribution of biological, psychological and socio-cultural influence on drug-taking behaviour are to be taken into consideration while going into the depth of the causation behind drug abuse. The personality and socio-cultural factors are to be much emphasized. Drug addiction is to be studied in the background of various familial background factors, the residential localities, educational status, cultural influence, rural and urban settings and other psycho-social factors.

The present book based on the research project sponsored by University Grants Commission on the problem of the 'prevalence of drug abuse among Delhi University Students: a study of some psycho-social concomitants' is the product of a highly scientific investigation carried on by Dr A.K. Sen, Professor of Psychology and the former Head of the Department of Psychology, University of Delhi and National Lecturer, UGC who has established his identity not only as a Professor of Psychology but also as a dedicated researcher in the field of psychology. One more name associated with this project is that of Dr Anis Ahmad (Project Associate). After going through the project report submitted by them, I feel that they have made a significant contribution towards understanding the genesis of drug abuse among the youth while analyzing various psycho-social factors as contributors to drug abuse. They have quenched the thirst of those researchers, professionals, academicians, social workers and government machinery who are very much interested to find out the relationship of drug-taking behaviour with various personalistic as well as socio-cultural factors. In this book the investigators have clearly shown that drug abuse is a multifaceted problem which needs multidimensional attack. They have intensively surveyed the prevalence rate of drug abuse among users and compared them with non-users, and further studied specific psycho-social concomitants producing drug-taking behaviour. They studied specifically the drug users and non-users groups of students belonging to general, medical, engineering and nursing discipline. An intensive effort has been made to identify the frequency of intake and types of drugs by these two groups. The study was conducted on 1600 students from different professional and non-professional colleges of Delhi University. The selected samples were studied with the help of a structured questionnaire and other standardized psychological tests. The list of drugs on which the users and non-users were compared in itself is the indicator of the pain taken by the investigators in the process of conducting the research. The study has been conducted on the students from whom the task of seeking information on the use of drugs is highly difficult, but the investigators successfully managed it.

The project report has been submitted in two volumes and the results have been presented itemwise in the form of tables and graphs which provide easy reading of the report. The plethora of research data generated by the attack on the problem of drug abuse from different angles, lies in store for the researchers to grapple with it, and its documentation is the outstanding feature of the present book on prevalence of drug abuse. In this respect it serves as one of the most comprehensive books of reference relating to the subject. The present volume on prevalence of drug abuse will provide valuable source material for future researches on the problem, on the one hand, and a valuable guidance to the educationists, social agencies, government machinery, counsellors and the university administrators who have to acknowledge their responsibility towards the solution of drug abuse exhibited by our youths, especially the students, who are the builders of our nation. The intake of drug by our youths will hinder with the expression of their creative talents especially when they have to compete with the rest of the world in the 21st century which demands youths enjoying a healthy body with a healthy mind. I can simply say that credit is to be given to the authors for successfully writing the book and providing enriched material in this regard which could be an excellent guide to all those who are interested in the prevention and the treatment of the drug abuse.

Vice-Chancellor
Nalanda Open University
and
Former Professor and Head,
Department of Psychology,
Patna University, Patna

Shamshad Hussain

PREFACE

Drug abuse is a great problem in every society throughout the globe. The question of how a free society should deal with drug abuse remains unsolved. The modern world seems unable to form a consensus or even a consistent attitude about the subject. It is important to know, what we mean by a drug. Some of the substances have medical uses, but they are not ordinary medicines. What distinguishes them is the fact that they act on the Central nervous system and are used to change thoughts, feelings, perceptions and behaviour. Among them are the opiates— heroin and morphine, the stimulants— amphetamine and cocaine, sedatives and tranquillizers like barbiturates, alcohol and tobacco. Since these drugs affect the mind, they are often called "psychoactive". Some drugs, especially alcohol and tobacco are not usually regarded as drugs. The other drugs which are termed as "narcotics" are known as "drug of abuse."

This research was aimed to find out the prevalence rate of drug abuse among the youth, why they take them and how to stop it. Initially a survey was conducted among 1600 students, and later on a comparison was made between the drug abusers and non-abusers, on some psycho-social concomitants.

This book is an outcome of the UGC sponsored project of which the first author was the Principal Investigator and the second author was a Research Associate. The authors are thankful to Dr N.K. Chadha, Reader, Dept. of Psychology, Delhi University, who at the initial stage was a co-investigator of this project. But due to his other pre-occupations and commitments, he could not make himself available throughout. Even then he has given us moral support and encouragement and we are grateful to him for this. We are also thankful to Dr Indu Arneja whose help and assistance was very useful in shaping the book in the present form. The authors are grateful to Prof Shamshad Hussain, Vice Chancellor, Nalanda

Open University for writing the 'Foreword' of the book. We also express our sincere gratitude to Professor Shamim Ahmad Ansari of the department of Psychology, Aligarh Muslim University, for his instant help and assistance, as and when we required. Thanks are also due to all those students who volunteered gladly to respond to a long questionnaire administered to them during data collection.

Professor Anima Sen who is no more with us had given her whole-hearted support and encouragement in our study. She was an exemplary research psychologist, a distinguished teacher and a warm-hearted noble person. Due to her sudden demise on the night of 9th August, 1995, a big vacuum has been created among her admirers and in the academic circle. We dedicate this book to the fond memory of Professor (Mrs.) Anima Sen.

A.K. Sen

Anis Ahmad

1

INTRODUCTION

In the fast changing scenario of the world, youths, especially students of the youthful age are considered to be the future assets of the family and the nation at large. These youngsters can contribute a lot for the welfare and the advancement of the family or nation in a truly global sense only if their energies and potentialities are channelized in the most appropriate and desired manner. On the contrary, if they indulge in undesirable activities like drug addiction which has become the most prevalent social evil in the present times, they can never utilize their potential and energies for self growth, family welfare as well as for the welfare and development of the nation. The prevalence of an alarming growth rate of drug addiction warrants us to take preventive steps for the proper utilization of human resources.

Since the earliest recorded times, drugs have been employed for mainly three different reasons — religious, recreational and medicinal. In ancient times, drugs were mainly used for the treatment of ailments and ritualistic ceremonies. During those periods, drug abuse was considered as the sign of enjoyment. The habit of addiction in India is evident from the eras of *Rigveda, Ramayana* and the *Mahabharata* and intoxicants were given numerous names as *'Soma Rasa'*, *'Madhu'*, etc. For example, alcohol and opium were both well-known in ancient Egyptian culture, while cannabis was commonly used in Hindu ceremonial rites as well as in Indian and Chinese medicine systems. Drug related problems, therefore, are not new. When the drugs were taken for treatment or enjoyment, they had not posed any problem but their excessive use in any form raised psycho-social problems not in India alone but also in nations all over the world.

The use of psychoactive, dependence producing substances for recreational, social and medicinal purposes probably dates back to prehistoric times. Though, the use of psychoactive drugs is not new in India, their widespread abuse is a balooning phenomenon. The day by day increasing trend of drug abuse and addiction in India has caused both public and scientific attention to be focused on it.

The World Health Organization has adopted the following definitions and usages for the dependence-producing drugs:

Drug : Any substance that, when taken into the living organism, may modify one or more of its function.

Drug dependence : A psychic state, and sometimes also physical, resulting from the interaction between a living organism and a drug, characterized by behavioural and other responses that always include a compulsion to take on a continuous or periodic basis in order to experience its psychic effects and sometimes to avoid the discomfort of its absence. In this state, tolerance may or may not be present when the person is dependent on more than one drug.

Drug abuse : The misuse of drugs may take the form of dependence or abuse. In traditional parlance, dependence signified psychological reliance on a particular drug, while addiction was reserved for psychological dependence, as indicated by withdrawal symptoms if the drugs were to be discontinued. Recently, however, drug dependence has come to denote both psychological and physiological dependence. The term drug abuse is used to indicate the excessive consumption of a drug, regardless of whether an individual is truly dependent on it. Of course, drug abuse often leads to drug dependence. Drug-abuse is defined as taking a drug for reasons other than medical, in an amount, strength, frequency or manner that damages the physical or mental functioning. The term itself conveys the notion of social disapproval and usually by self-administration of any drug in a manner that deviates from the approved medical or social patterns within a given culture *(Jaffe, 1991)*. Drug abuse is growing at an explosive rate and in just little over a decade it has spread its malevolent tentacles to almost every part of the globe surmounting almost all barriers of race, caste, creed, religion, sex, educational status, economic strata, etc, with astounding ease. Increasing evidences are pouring in to suggest that a large percentage of students are being "hooked on" dependence-producing drugs and have succumbed to the illusory panacea of drugs *(Jiloha & Munjal, 1985; Arneja & Sen, 1990).*

Substances may be abused for psychological, sociological or biological reasons. The biological reasons for abuse have been broadly classified into two categories: (i) a 'liking factor' and (ii) the effects of tolerance and physical dependence. The liking factor has been separated into two processes : mood elevation and relief from anxiety or tension. Physical dependence is an adaptive state that manifests itself by intense physical disturbances when the administration of the drug is suspended or when its action is affected by the administration of a specific antagonist. These disturbances, i.e., withdrawal or abstinence syndromes, are made up of specific arrays of symptoms and signs of psychic and physical nature that are characteristic for each drug type. These conditions are relieved by re-administration of the same drug or of another drug of similar pharmacological action within the same generic type. No overt manifestation of physical dependence is evident if an adequate dosage is maintained. Physical dependence is a powerful factor in reinforcing the influence of psychic dependence upon continuing drug use after attempted withdrawal.

Tolerance : Tolerance is an addictive state characterized by diminished responses to the same quantity of a drug or by the fact that a larger dose is required to produce the same degree of pharmacodynamic effect.

Cross-tolerance : Cross-tolerance is a phenomenon in which one drug is taken and tolerance develops not only to that drug, but also to other drugs of the same, or sometimes related type.

Often, tolerance to a drug develops in an individual when the same dosage produces decreased effects after repeated use. The degree of tolerance and the rate at which it is acquired depend on the specific drug, the person using it, and the frequency and magnitude of its use. Dosages of drugs that produce tolerance e.g. alcohol, barbiturates, and heroin, tend to be increased by persons using them as their tolerance to a particular drug increases. The mechanisms by which physiological tolerance is acquired are not fully understood. There is some evidence which shows that the central nervous system develops some degree of tolerance for various drugs; but, in addition, learning may play an important role in changing an individual's attitude towards a drug and his response to it after repeated use. Thus with some drugs, such as marijuana, the individual may learn to control some effects and maintain relatively normal functioning.

Drug Usage : New Trends

Recently, drug problems have become more varied, becoming both more intricate and more global in character. Natural drugs such as cannabis, cocaine, *khat* and opium, which had previously been used only within certain cultural settings and confined to traditional ways of life, have been increasingly exploited and have now reached epidemic levels.

Furthermore, synthetically manufactured drugs such as amphetamines, barbiturates, and a wide range of sedatives and tranquillizers have become more readily available in both licit and illicit markets.

One of the most important changes which have been noticed is that earlier drugs were primarily used by adults but now all types of drugs are being used by almost all people of pre-adolescence, adolescence, and post-adolescence ages. These people do not only primarily belong to minority groups or those living in poor social and economic conditions but come from middle, upper middle and upper classes.

Hypotheses on Drug Abuse Behaviour

Theories of drug abusing behaviours have been remarkedly diversed and problematical. *Lettieri (1978)* who classified them according to four criteria, such as: (1) psychological theories, (2) socio-psychological theories, (3) sociological theories and (4) naturalistic theories. A furthermore parsimonious reduction is possible, one that differentiates between a human's micro level (physiological and genetic) and macro level (environmental and grossly) behaviours. This reduction demonstrates that most theories of drug using behaviour attach only part of the total interaction, looking only at the behaviour, or only at the behaviour and the environment, or still only consider hereditary factors. All drug using theories or hypotheses can be differentiated according to phenotype and environment, and can be classified as phenotypic, phenoenvirotypic or genotypic.

Phenotypic Hypotheses

Phenotypic hypotheses are those primarily based on the visible characteristics of the group as contrasted with the underlying hereditary characteristics. These hypotheses include: psychological approaches which specify personality deficiencies, *Chein (1966)*; *Greeves (1974)* who speculates that drug dependent persons substitute drugs as their primary source of pleasure; *Crowley (1972)* who indicates that continued drug use can be explained in terms of the positive reinforcement afforded by pleasure and the negative reinforcement afforded by fear of pain from withdrawal. *Savitt (1963)* emphasizes returning to a regressive oral state as a factor in heroin addiction. The phenotypic category also includes *Grover's View (1939)* who pointed out in his theories that drugs are used to defend against aggressive and sadistic impulses; and *Wikler (1973)* who offers conditioning as the mechanism to explain addiction.

Phenoenvirotypic Hypotheses

Phenoenvirotypic hypotheses pertaining to drug use behaviours are based on both environmental factors and observed characteristics (phenotype) and encompass sociological and socio-psychological interpretations. These hypotheses include: *Weech (1966)* who views street addiction as a sanctuary from family disturbances; *Paschke (1970)* sees peer group influence as paramount; *Milkman and Frosch (1973)* speculate that individuals use drugs to cope with psychological distress; and *Blachly (1970)* pointed out that addiction as one of a variety of seductive behaviour where gratification must be immediate rather than diffused. *Hill (1962)* finds family disturbances interfering with the individual's development of independence instrumental to addiction and *Lindersmith (1947)* presents a pampered lifestyle as a factor in drug usage; *Cloward and Ohlin (1960)*, as a result of a study of delinquent gangs, support alienation as an antecedent condition in drug abuse while *Fort (1954)* suggests that overprotected early life experiences are factors perpetuating drug use later. *Seldin (1972)* finds pathological family environment as precipitating addiction and *Merton (1957)* determines that rejection of societal goals and societal means of goal attainment leads to addictive behaviour. *Cohen (1971)* concludes that the search for euphoria and for relief from psychological pain is a sustaining reason for individual involvement with addictive drugs.

Genotypic Hypotheses

Genotypic hypotheses emphasize the genetic composition of an individual and examine hereditary factors that exert a causative influence on development. These hypotheses include: *Jonas and Jonas (1977),* who view addiction in terms of overall evolutionary processes; *Bejerot (1972)* sees addiction as an artificially induced drive based on the biology of the brain's pleasure centres; *Weil (1972)* believes that drug taking is a motivator residing in neurological structures of the brain, which functions to alter consciousness; and *Dole and Nyswander (1967)* identified that addiction is the result of a metabolic dysfunction. One of the most important theories presented by *Frye (1980),* i.e., the socio-biological theory, stated that approaches leading to explanation of drug use behaviour have usually been clarified by assigning them to one of the branches of biology or the social sciences, causing an artificial dichotomy.

A new classification is needed, which differentiates or synthesizes according to phenotype, genotype and physical and cultural environments. In this context it could be generalized that drug abuse behaviour is a syndrome based on genetically adaptive behavioural patterns and is also a social behaviour with biological foundations. This is the root cause why a comprehensive theory of drug abuse behaviour must reflect the biological make-up and evolutionary past of humankind, and could be illustrated by the universally tried formula: P=G+Ef (P=Person, G=Genetic, Ef= Environmental factors) and it must relate to a general theory of behaviour. The socio-biological theory appears to fulfil these criteria and utilize descriptions, and hereditary and adaptive dimensions.

Sociocultural Aspects of Drug Abuse

Sociologists have already pointed out that social and environmental factors may determine drug use without the existence of any personal problems or interrelationships (which are difficulties) which explain the involvement. With reference to this context *Alistair (1985)* stated that the past decade has seen a move away from the assumed importance of psychological and socio-demographic variables in the development of drug use, and perceived that the social context of drug users (peer and family influences) and situational variables (drug availability, adolescent cultural values) are more influential in the development of dependency. He pointed out that the main social influences towards drug use relate to minority group state; parental loss, separation, disharmony or illness; low income; a state of deprivation peer group influence towards deviant subcultural activities; restricted opportunities for acceptable socialization; defective socializing influences; and easy drug availability, choice and cost.

Salmon & Salmon (1977) gave five predisposing social factors as: (i) urban area; (ii) masculine behavioural modes with a refutation of familial responsibility; (iii) anomie, with retreatist behaviour in response to failure in achieving social and cultural status, either in the straight or the criminal world; (iv) deficiencies in normal social opportunity structures, and (v) association with delinquent groups and consequent behavioural learning of deviancy.

Drug abuse is a psycho-socio-medical problem which needs to be treated in the entirety of the life situations of the addict. Researches have shown that drug abuse is a multifaceted and multidimensional problem. A variety of socio-economic factors which have been held responsible for this malady are familial discord, social ostracism, emotional insecurity, stress and strains of modern life, professional anxiety, erosion in social values and socio-economic changes currently sweeping national development along with simple curiosity of floating high and achieving dreamy pleasurable sensations. Another peculiar aspect of drug abuse is indulgence of the addict in antisocial activities including begging, borrowing or stealing money and other valuables from home and outside to sustain the supply of drugs without which the addict can no longer pull on. The crux of the situation is that a large majority of girl addicts can only afford drugs by indulging in prostitution. Further, the suicide rate amongst addicts is considerably higher as compared to general population *(Jaffe, 1985)*.

Prevention of Drug Trafficking : A Perspective of Drug Law Enforcement in India

India has a long history of control of drug abuse particularly over opium and cannabis. The problem of illicit trafficking was comparatively simple until the late seventies. Control was exercised under the Opium Act, 1857 and the Opium Act, 1878 in respect of all operations connected with the legal production, transport, inter-state movement, possession, distribution, warehousing, sale, etc., of opium, but to give effect to the Geneva Convention of 1925 the

Government enacted the Dangerous Drugs Act, 1930. It was a comprehensive legislation to extend controls over the entire range of narcotic drugs. Later, India became a signatory to Single Convention on Narcotic Drugs in 1961, The Convention of Psychotropic Substances of 1971 and the Amending Protocol of 1972. It maintained a strict system of control in the field of poppy cultivation and opium production for medical and scientific uses in accordance with the provisions of.the Single Convention of 1961. Moreover, the focus of international community on India as a transit country strengthened the resolve for taking firm legal and administrative measures to attack on the drug problem on all fronts. It was realized that the illicit supply and demand of drugs were interrelated and the problem transcended national frontiers. However, it was not only necessary to: (i) update the earlier laws on the subject and provide deterrent penalties; (ii) extend the control on psychotropic substances, the abuse of which had become noticeable; (iii) bring in cannabis within the ambit of the Central law, but that there should be (iv) legal obligation on the State for identification, treatment, rehabilitation and social reintegration of drug addicts. The Narcotic Drugs and Psychotropic Substances Act of 1985 was promulgated to achieve the above objectives. It was truly a historic legislation with regard to the scope and sweep of its provisions and deterrence against contraventions. (Courtesy: *Indian Express*)

Narcotic Drugs and Psychotropic Substances (NDPS) Act, 1985

The Government of India has taken a number of steps and launched several programmes administering the Narcotic Drugs and Psychotropic Substances Act, 1985. The NDPS Act which came into force w.e.f. 14.11.1985 consolidated and unified into a Sign Act all the provisions related to all narcotic drugs. The Act provided for regulation of cultivation of poppy, coca, cannabis, manufacture of drugs (potency for abuse), and other matters relating to possession, transport, trading and import/export, etc.

The salient features of the Act include enhanced scale of punishment for major offences (for example, trafficking); imposition of fine higher than the maximum fine prescribed for reasons to be recorded in the judgement. Provisions have also been made in the new Act that in the case of an addict, who is guilty of the offence of consumption, the court, instead of straightaway sentencing him to imprisonment, may release nim for undergoing medical treatment for de-addiction on his executing suitable bonds. Attempts, abetment, conspiracy and preparation to commit an offence is also made punishable. All offences have been made cognizable.

For repeated offences in respect of both the narcotic drugs and psychotropic substances (except item No. 3 of Table 1.1) the minimum punishment would be 15 years of rigorous imprisonment and a fine of Rs. 1.5 lakh and maximum punishment would be 30 years of rigorous imprisonment and a fine of Rs. 3 lakh.

The prescribed punishment for the various offences by NDPS Act, 1985 is presented in Table 1.1.

With the same end in view of a variety of educational programmes both through the formal system and the informal initiatives of people themselves are extended under the State patronage. To deal with problems related to drugs, requires a multidisciplinary approach.

TABLE 1.1

The Punishment Prescribed For The Various Offences By The NDPS Act, 1985

Sl. No.	*Description of the Offence*	*Minimum*		*Maximum*	
		Imprison-ment	*Fine*	*Imprison-ment*	*Fine*
1.	Trafficking (Internal)	10 yrs (RI)	Rs 1 lakh	20 yrs (RI)	Rs 2 lakh
2.	Trafficking	10 yrs (RI)	Rs 1 lakh	20 yrs (RI)	Rs 2 lakh
3.	Trafficking (internal) in respect of *Ganja*, and illegal cultivation, etc.	10 yrs	Rs 1 lakh	5 yrs (RI)	Rs 5000
4.	Trafficking (internal) in respect of cannabis other than *Ganja*.	10 yrs (RI)	Rs 1 lakh	20 yrs (RI)	Rs 2 lakh

Note : RI = Rigorous Imprisonment

A high level Indian delegation also had attended the International Conference on Drug Abuse and Illicit Trafficking held at Vienna from 17-26th June, 1987 to control the drug situation in India under the leadership of Minister of State for Finance. The strategy suggested by the conference was quite comprehensive and covers all the four areas involved in fighting drug-abuse:

1. The prevention and reduction of illicit demand.
2. The control of supply.
3. Action against illicit trafficking. and
4. Treatment and rehabilitation.

Comprehensive and stringent action has been taken against items II and III of the preceding para by the Narcotic Drugs and Psychotropic Substances Act, 1985 which has further been intensified with the enactment of Prevention of Illicit Trafficking in Narcotic Drugs and Psychotropic Substances Act, 1988 providing for preventive detention of drug traffickers and the Narcotic Drugs and Psychotropic Substances (Amendment) Act, 1989, providing for capital punishment for drug traffickers in certain cases. Action against item No. 4 above is being taken by the Ministry of Health and Family Welfare and Ministry of Welfare as well as by the State governments and non-voluntary organizations. For item No. 1 action is being taken by the mass media, political parties, non-voluntary organizations and student activists. Fortunately, public awareness of the problem has immensely increased and a strong public opinion has been generated on the need for concerted action to arrest the situation.

Prevention Strategies of Drug Abuse

Prevention, treatment and rehabilitation are the three corner-stones in the comprehensive management of problem of drug-abuse. The overall strategy for drug abuse prevention is based on an interdisciplinary, integrated and coordinated action particularly involving active cooperation of the family and the community, and attention to aspects of social environments in which drugs are abused as also developing preventive policies at community level. We can also say that drug-abuse is to be tackled in the social context. As drug abuse is more prevalent among youths hence the source of its introduction and the reasons for their indulgence particularly friends circle and family background should be thoroughly probed *(Jiloha, 1990)*. Moreover, there are various non-pharmacological remedial measures namely, psychotherapy, group therapy, individual therapy, hypnosis, yoga, meditation, educational programmes pertaining to awareness of drug misuse, electroconvulsive therapy, socio-economic welfare support, religious conversion, etc, can be very much helpful to control, prevent or cure problems of drug abuse. Drugs also generate feelings of fear, anxiety, insecurity, inadequacy and produce social isolation leading to chronic loneliness and self-destructive tendencies. In addition counselling centres and de-addiction centres should be setup in every school and college for creating more community awareness about drug abuse. Moreover, posters, slides and documentaries would have to be developed. Anti-narcotic students camps, poster designing competitions, debates, discussions and dramas would result in active student participation in anti-drug programmes. This requires increased communication between universities and media personnel. In conclusion it may be said that an overall effort should be made for utilizing all means to prevent drug abuse among students. For the achievement of these objectives, different programmes of formal and informal nature will have to be organized, and all available sources, organizations and agencies, schools, colleges, universities and mass media will have to be involved for the prevention of drug abuse among youths in general and students in particular.

2

DIFFERENT DRUGS AND THEIR USES

In the olden days, drugs were used for the treatment of ailments and in ritual ceremonies. But excessive use of any drug in any form raises various psycho-social problems. Drug-addiction and drug habituation both involve repeated consumption of a natural or synthetic drug. In the case of habituation, there is a desire but not a compulsion to continue taking the drug. There is little tendency to increase the dosage and there is some psychological but no physiological dependence. In the case of addiction and habituation also the drugs are used unofficially, but there is no existence of medical reasons. Drug abuse is, however, different in the sense that the person may not have developed physical or psychological dependence. The drug may be taken very occasionally to overcome some stresses or to feel free from mental or physical fatigue.

Generally, drugs are categorized according to their chemical structure, pharmacological action or chemical use. Here an attempt is made to classify the drugs according to their historical origins and social uses.

(i) One of the most common groups of naturally derived substances are primarily used for recreational purposes. These are tobacco, alcohol, tea and coffee.

(ii) There is another group of naturally derived substances, of great antiquity and of varying potency, which was originally used for some therapeutic and religious purposes. Substances that appeared to relieve pain, cure disease, alleviate anxiety, and produce a mystical and/or an ecstatic state are the opiates, cannabis, cocaine, peyote, and mescaline.

(iii) Recently, research and development has produced a variety of drugs originating from natural substances or totally synthesized by commercial pharmaceutical houses for the treatment of various medical ailments. The opium derivatives such as morphine and heroin, as well as synthetic analgesics such as methadone, certain anti-depressants, tranquillizers and anti-anxiety drugs, etc., belong to this group.

(iv) Drugs have also been developed for other purposes which may affect the brain. These are amphetamines, LSD, etc., developed as an analeptic or restorative.

Natural Drugs

Caffeine and Tobacco

Caffeine and tobacco are most widely consumed psychoactive substances in the world. The history of these substances illustrates the triumph of what might be called the pleasure principle over strong initial opposition. The introduction of tobacco after the early voyages of discovery prompted European countries to enact laws restricting or forbidding its use. In England, restriction was also imposed to limit the use of tobacco, apparently, for preventing the deterioration of the working classes. Similarly, introduction of tea in England met with violent opposition, in many respects reminiscent of the opposition to marijuana, known in the argot as tea. Since both nicotine and caffeine are used worldwide and have become part of the day-to-day life, they are commonly considered non-drugs.

Meanwhile, on the dependence producing affect of these drugs, both caffeine and tobacco are clearly dependence-producing substances with a capacity to cause physical harm to the users. According to World Health Organization Tech. Rep. Series No. 516 (1973) — "tobacco, however, unlike the types of severe dependence producing drugs, produces relatively little stimulation or depression of the central nervous system, or disturbances in perception, mood, thinking, behaviour or motor functions." In a study conducted by *Singh (1978)*, 95% drug abuser subjects were tobacco-smokers. Similar results have also been reported by *Mohan and Arora (1976)*.

Apart from its high prevalence rate, tobacco smoking is also the medium for taking so many dependence producing drugs like marijuana, hashish, *ganja* and lately smack. Marijuana is prepared from Mexican variety of hemp. Hashish is prepared from resin separated from the plant and synonymous to *charas*. *Charas* is the resinous matter collected from the leaves and flowering tops of the female plants. In India, the cultivated plant does not yield sufficient resin which can be collected separately. *Charas* was formerly imported from Central Asia and formed an important article of trade between India and Central Asia. Hashish is mainly used in the Middle East and in the Arab countries. *Ganja* consists of the dried flowering and or fruiting tops of the cultivated cannabis plant which are coated with a resinous exudence chiefly from the glandular hairs, in consequence of being deprived of the opportunity of setting seeds. One of the most common drugs, 'smack', is extracted from the hemp plant.

It is essentially significant to mention that in India, three narcotics, *bhang, ganja* and *charas* are obtained from the hemp plant. These drugs are different from each other in terms of the methods of preparation and types of plants used for extraction. Hemp drugs act chiefly on the cerebrum. The drug causes in the addict the desire to recapture the pleasurable euphoric state into which the drug lifts him. There is no physiological disturbance on the withdrawal of the drug. Smoking of the drug, if continued causes intoxication and loss of self control. The drugged person becomes talkative and jovial, has less control over himself and passes into a sort of delirium. Hemp drugs are therefore called euphorics, exhilarants, deliriants and hypnotics. Dependence on them is mainly of psychological nature. It is regarded as habit forming rather than an addictive drug.

Opium and its Derivatives

Opium (Greek for juice) is produced from the milky exudate of the unripe seed pods of the poppy plant. This plant is chiefly cultivated in India, Iran, Afghanistan, Pakistan, Turkey, China and in South-East Asian countries and grows wild in Southern Europe and in England. The poppy capsules have sedative and euphoric effect and are taken in the form of beverage prepared by soaking and boiling the capsules in water. Today, opium derivatives are still important to medical practitioners for use as medicine. The primary use of it is for relief of pain, but it is also used for the treatment of diarrhoea, coughs, dysentery and other digestive ailments. Opium is prepared by thickening the milk extracted from the unripe capsules of poppy plant and can be eaten or smoked. *Madak* and *Chandu* are the two crude preparations of opium which are smoked. Smoking of opium initially produces euphoric symptoms. The senses become keen because there is a sense of elation and a sense of superiority.

Permanent use of opium makes a person dull and drowsy. The effects of taking poppy capsules are similar to those produced by opium but are somewhat milder. There is a gradual transition from elation to depression. There is loss of memory and also loss of sense of time and space.

Morphine

This is the most important among all natural drugs which is capable of producing sedation and relieving pain. This is also a derivative of opium. Analgesia, drowsiness, change in mood, and mental clouding are the effects which are produced by morphine. The use of opium derivatives over a period of time usually results in a physiological craving for the drug. The time required to establish the drug habit, however, varies. Gradually, the user of opium derivatives builds up a tolerance to the drug, resulting in larger amounts for the desired effects.

Heroin

Heroin is a simple derivative of morphine. Scientists concerned with the addictive properties of morphine hypothesized that one part of the morphine molecule might be responsible for its analgesic properties and another for its addictiveness. An analgesic is a drug that alleviates pain without inducing unconsciousness. Thus, at about the turn of the century, it was discovered that if morphine was treated by an inexpensive and readily available chemical called acetic anhydride, it could be converted into another powerful analgesic called heroin. Leading scientists during the time agreed with the merits of heroin, and the drug came to be widely prescribed in place of morphine for pain relief and related medicinal purposes.

During the 1960s there was a rapid increase in the use of heroin— the peak year was 1969 when there were an estimated 1,50,000 or more addicts in New York city alone, and some 3,00,000 in the USA as a whole and public attention was focused on the "heroin epidemic" *(Bazell, 1973; Greene & Dupont, 1974)*. However, as a result of strict control by federal and local authorities, programmes of public education, and more effective methods of detection and treatment, heroin addiction markedly decreased during the 1970s. Beginning from 1974 onwards again there was an increased tendency for heroin usage which spread from large cities to rural communities *(Dupont, 1975; Wilson, 1975)*.

However, in some instances withdrawal is an agonizing and perilous experience. The initial symptoms usually include: a running nose, tears in the eyes, perspiration, restlessness, increased respiration rate, and an intensified desire for the drug.

Heroin is very harmful for health. If the heroin user injects too much, his respiration is slowed, which can cause coma and death. In 1969 in New York city— a peak year of heroin addiction in the United States, there were more than 900 deaths associated with heroin usage, 224 of which were of teenagers who died from overdoses or heroin-related infections *(Abelson, 1970)*.

Cannabis

Drug preparation from the hemp plant vary widely in quality and potency, depending on the type, climate, soil, cultivation, and method of preparation.

Preparation of the hemp drug comes in three grades, identified by Indian names called *bhang, ganja* and *charas*. It produces intense anxiety, and depression as well as delusions and hallucinations.

Because of their low cost and easy availability the cannabis drugs are more frequently used than other drugs. The use of these drugs by ascetics and religious mendicants is not uncommon. They are used in rituals performed in some of the Hindu temples, and during festivals like Shivaratri, Holi and Diwali. Their use is fairly widespread.

Khat

Khat is of African origin and is mainly grown on the highlands of Ethiopia. In India, it is grown in Mysore and some parts of Maharashtra. Sometimes, it is consumed in the form of an infusion. Its use reduces fatigue, and hunger and has a soothing effect. Its continuous use seems to have adverse effect on the higher brain activities and causes disturbances of schizophrenic character.

Alcohol

Despite the publicity given during the 1960s to a few drugs, notably heroin and opium, alcohol has long been and continues to be the most widely used and popular of the "mind-bending" drugs. The technical name of the drug in alcoholic beverages is ethanol, or ethyl alcohol, popularly, it is known simply as alcohol.

Alcohol has a marked effect on the central nervous system. It is not a 'stimulant' as long believed, but a primary and continuous depressant. Alcohol produces psychic dependence of varying degrees from mild to strong. Physical dependence develops slowly. Alcohol is essential to the treatment of certain diseases. Drinking several cups of coffee can counteract the effects of alcohol. According to current concept, alcoholism is considered a disease and alcohol a 'disease agent' which causes acute and chronic intoxication, cirrhosis of the liver, toxic psychosis, pancreatis, cardiomyopathy, and peripheral neuropathy. Moreover, alcohol is an important etiologic factor in suicide, automobile and other accidents, and injuries and deaths due to violence *(Park and Park, 1985)*.

Coca

This plant does not grow in India but the drug cocaine derived from this plant is smuggled into the country, mainly from the countries of the far eastern region. Cocaine is used primarily in different States in India, like UP, Bihar, Bengal and Punjab. This particular drug is usually taken with betel leaf. Like other drugs mentioned earlier cocaine also produces euphoric sensations. It has a marked effect in relieving fatigue and mental depression. It produces almost complete loss of appetite though an intense feeling of thirst is experienced by an addict. Unlike other drugs it does not produce drowsiness and sleep.

Manufactured Drugs

There are various types of manufactured drugs like :

Amphetamine

Amphetamine and cocaine have chemical effects that stimulate or speed up central nervous system activity.

The earliest amphetamine to be introduced, Benzedrine, or amphetamine sulphate was first synthesized in 1927 and became available in drug stores in the early 1930s as an inhalent to relieve stuffy noses. During World War II, military interest was aroused in the stimulating effects of these drugs, and they were used by both allied and German soldiers to ward off fatigue *(Jarvik, 1967)*. Similarly, amphetamines became more popular among civilians and came to be widely used by night workers, long-distance truck drivers, students cramming for examinations, and athletes striving to improve their performance.

The amphetamines are sometimes used medically for curbing the appetite when weight reduction is desired. It is also used for relieving fatigue and maintaining alertness for sustained periods of time. Amphetamines alleviate mild feelings of depression. Similarly, amphetamines are also used for individuals suffering from narcolepsy— (a disorder in which the subject cannot prevent himself from continually falling asleep during the day) as well as for the treatment of hyperactive children. Like other drugs, the effects of amphetamines vary with the type, dosage and length of time they are taken, and the physical and psychological state of the individual user. Although amphetamines are not considered to be physiologically addictive, the body does build up tolerance to them very rapidly.

Barbiturates

In the 1850s, new chemical compounds came on the scene known as bromides. They immediately became popular as sedatives and were taken by millions of people. But with use came abuse, and the excessive consumption of bromides resulted in toxic psychoses involving delusions, hallucinations, and a variety of neurological disturbances, which for a time became a leading cause of admission to mental hospitals *(Jarvik, 1967)*. Misuse of bromides waned in the 1930s, when more powerful sedatives, called barbiturates, were introduced *(Coleman, 1982)*. As treatment for insomnia, depression and anxiety, barbiturates rapidly became one of the most prescribed and abused drugs in medicine. Barbiturates have their legitimate medical uses, though they are extremely dangerous drugs commonly associated with both physiological and psychological dependence as well as with lethal overdoses *(American Psychiatric Association, 1974)*. In addition, excessive use of barbiturates leads to a variety of undesirable side-effects, including sluggishness, slow speech, impaired comprehension and memory, motor incoordination, and depression.

Lysergic Acid Diethylamide (LSD)

In around 1950, LSD was introduced into the United States for purposes of research as well as to ascertain whether it might have medical or therapeutic uses. LSD is a chemically synthesized substance first discovered by the Swiss chemist Hoffman in 1938

(Coleman, 1982). It has strong hallucinogenic properties and is an odourless, colourless and tasteless drug. LSD can produce intoxication with an amount smaller than a grain of salt. It is generally believed that LSD is used to increase sensitivity, mystic experiences and better understanding of the universe. A sizeable number of painters, writers, and composers, used the drug not only for their personal growth but also as a means of creating more original and meaningful works of art. However, it may be mentioned here that there is no scientific evidence which testifies that LSD enhances creative activity. In fact, under the direct influence of LSD, the drawings of one well-known American painter showed progressive deterioration. Later, when asked if he felt his LSD experience had improved his creativity, he replied in the negative *(Rinkel, 1966)*.

3

PSYCHOLOGICAL ASPECTS OF DRINKING AND ALCOHOLISM

Drinking, in drug abuse, refers to consuming of alcohol or its habitual or excessive consumption. Drinking and Alcoholism are oftenly considered as related but distinct phenomena. The use of alcoholic beverages by almost all societies over recorded history as a stimulant, anesthetic, social lubricant, and ceremonial substance is well known. Ingestion of alcohol may be normal or pathological, here the problem of definition starts. There is moderate drinking, acceptable in many but not all human groups; excessive drinking, for example, intoxication with behaviour problems associated with its practice; and there is alcoholism. Long time ago, the definition of alcoholism stated that "alcoholism is a psychologic dependence on or a psychological addiction to ethanol, manifested by the inability of the alcoholic consistently to control either the start of drinking or its termination once started...." *(Keller, 1962)*. Loss of control is the Pathognomic symptom here, and the definition specifies for the epidemiologist those behaviours that will permit him to define the alcoholic as it marked repetitive drinking as well as the ill effects on the drinker's health or on his social or economic functioning.

Drinking behaviour is oftenly interpreted in terms of different theoretical systems in psychology, for example, drinking has been viewed as a reducer of fear and conflict, by behaviourists, or as a dissolver of the superego, by psychoanalysts. Some studies of the influence of alcohol on human behaviour are being viewed as a wedge into related areas of knowledge.

Knowledge of the effects of alcohol on learning efficiency or motor coordination may be considered data about learning efficiency or motor coordination itself, about general drug effects, or about individual differences in response. The relationship of deviant drinking behaviour to human misery, personal and social, gives some insight into the dynamics of psychic pain and how ways of coping are passed on and learned. It is very interesting to point out that in some social groups and societies, such as nineteenth-century European Jewish Communities, alcohol may serve to reinforce social organisation. In other groups, alcohol may hasten the processes of disorganization and deculturation, the example of many North American Indian tribes is well known. Alcohol has been used occasionally as an instrument to achieve the submission of and control over others.

It is obviously clear that the term 'drinking' seems simple enough: an organism ingests an alcoholic beverage. But as a behavioural term, it includes many related aspects. In describing drinking behaviour one needs to know the kind and amount of beverage ingested and the circumstances of ingestion, such as how rapidly, with whom, how diluted, or whether drinking before or during meals, etc. . The term drinking encompasses the determination of the alcohol level produced by the drinking; the effects on efficiency, mood, and social interaction; the past experiences of the drinker and the drinking symptoms of the social group.

The psychological aspects of drinking are to be pointed out here to a review of research on the behavioural effects of alcohol on individual organisms.

There is a vast literature available on animal subjects and the effects of alcohol on their behaviour. Often, these are studies of alcohol effects in classical or operant - conditioning producers, reaction time and maze behaviour, but there have also been many laboratory reports, demonstrating increased voluntary consumption of alcohol under different experimental conditions, such as vitamin deficiency or stress, as well as some reports of laboratory work demonstrating genetic strain differences in alcohol preference. The term "experimental alcoholism" to describe these studies was criticised by the World Health Organization, Expert Committee on Alcohol (1954) which expressed the opinion that the phenomenon of alcoholism was closer to experiments dealing with "the relief by alcohol of experimentally induced neurotic manifestations in animals." "Such experiments include studies of experimenter induced conflicts and stress and of experimental neurosis." Whether such experiments relate to alcoholism or to the relief afforded by alcohol in every day, non-pathological social drinking may be a legitimate question, but there was another warning not to go too far in generalizing from the responses to alcohol of the animal in laboratory-generated stress to the complex, socially patterned drinking behaviour of the human subject.

There was a quite large amount of laboratory experimentation during the first four decades of this century on the effects of alcohol on different psychological variables. These have been summarized and evaluated in a monograph by *Jellinek* and *McFarland (1940)*. Experiments were grouped under these headings: Chronaxy, reflexes, sensations, perception and attention, simple reaction time, muscular strength and coordination, miscellaneous tests of dexterity and skill, learning and simple learned performances, memory, the associative functions, judgment , reasoning and intelligence, volition, emotion and personality. The generalization made from the authors' analysis of the experiments was that "alcohol has a depressing effect on all psychological functions yet measured, and .... such stimulation as has been reported for some psychological variables is a pseudostimulation." The reviewers also concluded that "the simple psychological functions are less affected by alcohol than the complex ones."

These conclusions are now being under critical reexamination and challenge. There is some evidence that small amounts of alcohol may in some task situations have a facilitating effect. It turns out too, that inferences about 'Pseudostimulation' are based on a melange of psychology and neurology, if behaviour or performance improves with alcohol. The argument is that such improvement occurs because cortical inhibitions are disinhibited by the alcohol. But studies of behaviour need to be described in behavioural and not in neurological terms, particularly not in oversimplified neurological terms that have been superseded by newer concepts of cerebral activity. As has been mentioned earlier, alcohol in small and moderate amounts is frequently a behavioural depressant but may— under some conditions, for some tasks, for some individuals—act as a facilitator *(Lisansky, 1964)*.

Experimental study of the effects of alcohol on emotional behaviour and the relationship of such effects to personality variables is in its infancy. There has been found some research suggesting that individual characteristics related to the effects of alcohol may be a subject's general adjustment, his introversive or extroversive tendencies, his past experience with alcohol, and his familiarity with a task. Interestingly enough, when people are asked to report their subjective feelings about how alcohol affects them, they almost invariably reply in terms of stimulating effects. This is indeed whether the people are laboratory subjects or participants in surveys. Experiments involving groups and the effects of alcohol on the emotional behaviour of individuals drinking together have been conducted by the Finnish Foundation for Alcohol studies. The limited number of group studies to date report increases in aggressive behaviour, in the sexual content of fantasies, and in emotionality of behaviour generally.

Etiology of Alcoholism

When we refer to "etiology" or "treatment", we speak of alcoholism *perse* as it presents itself in the industrialized, urbanized countries. Alcoholism is also viewed by many countries as a disease or a symptom of a disease process, and the concepts of etiology and treatment relate to this view. To perceive the most extreme of alcohol problems, alcoholism, as a disease requires a kind of mental health viewpoint not universal in the medical profession or welfare agencies, to say nothing of the lay public. It is a deviant behaviour, and as such it is seen by many as immorality, weakness of will, perversity, or a bad habit.

Physiopathological Theories

Etiological theories have been primarily physiopathological or psychopathological. Among physiopathological theories, there are explanations in terms of allergy, brainpathology, biochemical substances, nutritional deficiencies, and glandular disorder. These theories have still not gained more than limited acceptance. One of the major problems has been the difficulty of demonstrating that the particular physiopathological condition offered as the cause actually predated the onset of alcoholism. Generally, it has been bared on the condition of patients with longstanding alcoholism.

The World Health Organization (WHO), Expert Committee on Alcohol (1954) placed alcohol " in a category of its own, intermediate between addiction producing and habit-forming drugs." It is very important to note that the questions of alcohol and physical dependence or craving, alcohol and withdrawal, and alcohol and tolerance changes have not been solved and are still in debate.

Craving, withdrawal, and tolerance are now being considered as the criteria of addiction.

Psychopathological Theories

Psychopathological theories play an important role in the area of drug abuse, *Jellinek (1960)* divided into those viewing alcoholism as the illness and those viewing it as a symptom of illness. This distinction is the common view that some personality deviation or difficulty in socio-psychological development is a necessary condition of alcoholism. The psychoanalytic view emphasized "the oral and narcissistic premorbid personality," and various thinkers, theorizing from clinical data, have written of passivity, self-destruction, guilt, infantile traits, anxiety, and oral regression. The research survey of literature has been scanned and few scientists, viz; *Zwerling & Rosenbaum (1959) and Lisansky (1960),* were recorded. There has been a debate as to whether there is a single psychological predisposition, several such predispositions, or whether, indeed, any personality is vulnerable. Psychological test research has failed to turn up a single "alcoholic type". Psychological-clinical research with emphasis on social as well as psychological data about subjects and on behavioural criteria for differentiating among alcoholics might yet make a contribution. There has been some speculation by psychologists about how alcoholism develops whether it is a result of the reinforcement involved in reduction of fear, conflict, and tension. Very little has been written about the function alcohol serves in solving conscious and unconscious emotional needs. Therefore, psychopathology may be a necessary but not a sufficient causal explanation of alcoholism.

Socio-psychological Theories

Socio-psychological theories refer that one needs to know not only about individual tensions and frustrations but also about the group methods coping and its attitudes towards and perception of alcohol. *Jellinek (1960)* has offered a hypothesis relating to a society's degree of acceptance of "large daily alcohol consumption" and the psychological vulnerability of individuals. It seems that the same psychological vulnerability that predisposes towards alcoholism not only in Europe and America but have occupied place in Asia too.

It is undoubtedly a fact that there is no all embracing explanation of alcoholism in sight, but if one begins with a distinction between alcoholism and problems related to alcohol, if one is aware of the need for a classification of variants within the diagnosis of alcoholism, and if one is willing to include physiological, psychological, and social variables in an explanation of etiology, some ground is cleared. There is, probably, no theory which can ever account for all the problems men have with alcohol.

Drinking and alcoholism are important phenomena related to pressing problems in the psychological aspects. Those researchers who should have priority in research development, firstly consider the basic research on the effects of alcohol on mood, feelings, emotional response, and group behaviour and, secondly, a meaningful classification of the alcoholisms, probably in behavioural terms should be objectively defined, that could be used internationally and which may definitely lead to an understanding of the different etiologies and most effective treatments.

4

SOCIAL ASPECTS OF DRINKING AND ALCOHOLISM

Earlier, *Donald Horton (1943)* pioneered the first systematic cross-cultural study of drinking patterns in a report on the functions of alcohol in primitive societies. In his work he offered an eloquent plea for intensifying systematic research on drinking behaviour and for moving towards the goal of incorporating empirical findings into a general theory of the social and psychological functions of alcohol. After that the systematic study of drinking behaviour has proceeded at an accelerated pace in various branches of social science. But it cannot be said that the research has still produced the general theory which Horton had in mind. We shall, first consider here, some of the more general findings of comparative studies of drinking in primitive societies and of sociological and related studies of drinking in complex societies.

Primitive Societies' Drinking

Horton's research was one of the view that patterns of drinking behaviour are determined by the interrelations of psychological and cultural variables and, more specifically, the proposition that the primary function of alcoholic beverages in all societies is the reduction of anxiety. Horton also emphasized the other functions of alcohol as well as the seeming paradox that drinking may not be anxiety - reducing where social controls give rise to powerful and inhibiting counter anxieties. The basic notion of anxiety reduction is to a larger complex of psychocultural assumptions. *Horton (1943)* also derived some important theorems, enabling indirect tests of his basic proposition on a sample of 56 culturally distinct societies thought to represent a cross-section of primitive societies throughout the world.

The basic reason was that, drinking tends generally to be accompanied by the release of aggressive and sexual impulses, all societies must to some extent inhibit expression of these impulses, and to reduce impulse-anxiety through alcohol is, in effect, to release the inhibition. Moreover, the strength of the drinking response which Horton indexed by "the degree of insobriety", was thought to vary from culture to culture.

It is to be pointed out that the most dramatic of Horton's findings, however, related to the deduction that the strength of the drinking response varies directly with the general level of anxiety, which is an expression of the state of the total social structure and especially of the economy patterns of drinking behaviour: Horton also proposed a generalized qualitative sketch of three distinctive drinking patterns as he found in different parts of the world, which are expressions of the similarity in the crucial psychocultural variables seen as systems. The first pattern is associated with societies having high subsistence anxiety, strong belief in sorcery, weak sexual restraints, and coordinate social control. The second pattern occurs where the belief in sorcery is absent or relatively unimportant but where subsistence anxiety is also high and the anxiety motive too strong to be countered by sexual anxieties. It is, interestingly, to be pointed out here that Horton made no attempt to characterize the control of aggression in these societies but assumed from the unimportance of sorcery a minimum of motivation and thus little need for control. In the third pattern of drinking behaviour, Horton pointed out that fear and restraint in drinking are predominant, sometimes even extending to a complete taboo on alcoholic beverages. This sketch of patterns was not intended as exhaustive, but it offers the nucleus of a typology of patterns that have recurred with some frequency in primitive societies on a world-wide basis.

In addition to the above mentioned context, it is necessary to point out that a note of challenge to Horton's basic proposition on anxiety reduction was sounded in a cross-cultural study by *Field (1962),* who used Horton's original sample of primitive societies but extended the investigation to include variables not previously considered. Mentioning the highly inferential nature of Horton's measures of anxiety, Field introduced new indexes of "fear", which were thought to be more direct reflections of levels of anxiety, and found no consistent correlation with "extent of drunkenness". In his reconsideration, the relationship between subsistence insecurity and extent of drunkeness seemed more indicative of differences in economy, and hence in social organisation, than of strikingly different levels of anxiety. Consequently, Field abandoned Horton's anxiety reduction view in favour of exploring further the relations between social organization and drunkenness in primitive societies. Although, on the other hand, *Snyder (1964)* does not share Field's apparent dismissal of the role of anxiety in drinking, important relations between drunkenness and social organization which are suggested by his research. Generalizing his findings, Field proposed a distinction between "corporate" and "personal" types of social organization as the principal determinant of sobriety of drunkenness in primitive societies.

Ceremonial Usage and Solidarity

The extensive ceremonial usage of alcohol among primitive people has been studied by *Klausner (1964)* in a comparative study of 48 societies. He classified ceremonies in terms of their underlying meaning and characteristic form, according to the basic problems on which the center and the means employed, whether exorcism, scapegoating sacrifice, prayer, or other. Klausner, in his study, found no regular bond between ceremonial usage and sobriety but even noted a tendency, at the cultural level, for usage in religious ceremonies to be associated with heavy drinking in nonreligious situations. The findings also pointed out a connection between heavy drinking in nonreligious situations and the use of alcohol in sacrifice, especially when religious ceremonies were oriented toward "moral integration and control of the human world". Regardless of the ceremonial orientation, alcohol was more likely to be used in conjunction with sacrifice than with any other religious means. To account for cultural cases in which there was virtually no drinking beyond the boundaries of ceremonial situations, Klausner suggested in the light of the ancient symbolic equation of life-giving power, blood, and alcohol that when blood is considered holy, its symbolic equivalent alcohol, will not be drunk heavily in secular situations.

Drinking and Alcoholism in Complex Society

Important attempts to describe the functions of drinking in complex society have been rare in the writings of social scientists:- An exception is *Selden Bacon's (1945)*, essay depicting a large, highly specialized society as broadly "anomic... characterized by rapid change, lack of normative integration, compartmentalized social controls, the paradox of heightened individualism and functional interdependence, intense competition, mobility, and impersonality." The social value of alcohol is presumably enhanced in this context not only because it affords relief for tension-ridden individuals but also because it offers a needed mechanism of social integration, and the absence of generally held drinking norms conducive to extremes of drinking. This is a setting that also seems likely to precipitate rapid deterioration and isolation of the person who is prone to excessive drinking and also to lend drinking a greater individualistic significance than, it is likely to have in better integrated societies. In continuation with this, few studies were recorded, as the research of *Richard Jessor and Others (1963)* has established connections between extreme drinking and peaks of "anomie" - both in the sense of dissociation of cultural goals and means and in terms of simple break down in normative consensus. Excessive drinkers have also been found, in a scattering of studies, to exhibit signs of anomie and alienation. Alcoholics and incipient alcoholics, as studied by *Ralph G Connor (1962)* and *Peter Park (1962)*, evidenced difficulty in structuring their social roles in accordance with the role requirements of an impersonal complex society. The cosmopolitanism of the new middle classes *(Stone, 1962)* apparently supports a relatively permissive drinking norm, and thus abstinence has undergone devaluation in its status connotations. In a general sense, our culture has become dependent on alcohol as a social lubricant and a means of reducing tension - it is the "drug of choice." Thus numerous investigators have pointed to the role of sociocultural as well as physiological and psychological factors in the high rate of alcohol abuse and alcoholism among Americans as *Coleman (1982)* pointed out in his book.

It is of interest to note the conclusions of *Pliner and Cappell (1974)* concerning the reinforcing effects of social drinking in our society, in which liquor has come to play an almost ritualistic role in promoting gaiety and pleasant social interaction. It is also relevant to note that alcoholism is a major problem in two of the World's super powers - the United States and the Soviet Union.

But while there are many reasons why people drink, as well as many conditions that predispose them to and re-inforce drinking behaviour; the factors that result in a person's becoming an alcoholic are still unknown.

5

PSYCHOPHARMACOLOGY

This is one of the most important emerging aspects of drugs. Psychopharmacology is a relatively new scientific word, the interactive effects of drugs and behaviour are perhaps as old as man himself on earth. This presentation explains contemporary interest in Psychopharmacology and also emphasizes the social research frontiers. But it does not attempt to describe the emerging body of human and animal research results or the treatment aspects of drugs. In spite of focus on a number of individual and social factors relating to the effects of drugs. These factors are complex and generally poorly identified and weakly conceptualized. The ramifications of the questions lead one to consideration of the pathways of activity in the nervous system, the complexities of biochemical analysis, the assessment of human performance in laboratory or stimulated situations, the management of patients, and the social matrix in which all of human behaviour is embedded.

Drug utilization for health, religious, or individual purposes is one of the many primary human behaviours in a wide variety of cultures. Drugs thus constitute an almost universally present element to human social behaviour, and one to which individual reinforcement, social training, and private meaning are attached.

Although, the term "Psychopharmacology" has been used with increasing frequency over the past few years, the concept is by no means new to psychology. Various studies have been conducted to find out the effects of drugs on the behaviour of animals since in the nineteenth century, and the classic investigations of the effects of caffeine on human behaviour were carried out by *Hollingworth (1912)* in the first decade of the twentieth century. This series of studies embodied many of the aspects of good design and may still have value as a model for analysis of the effects of drugs on human behaviour.

Currently dramatic expansion of interest in psychopharmacology as a special area was considered in early 1950s. In its early phases it was a product of the joint action of pharmacologists and psychiatrists in their attempts at modification of the behaviour of psychiatric patients. Since the early 1950s, when drugs such as reserpine and chlorpromazine were introduced, the list of compounds has grown, although some main questions surround these drugs and their utilization.

Any real understanding of drugs that affect behaviour depends upon the development of adequate theory relating to biochemical or pharmacological events to behavioural events. *Callway and Stone (1960)* have examined the nature of theory in this area. On the biochemical side they find that the problem is formidable and aggravated by the lack of appropriate behavioural referents. Theories proposed by behavioural-scientists may greatly oversimplify the underlying biological complexities. On the other hand, theories constructed by biochemists and pharmacologists may be naive about the behavioural complexities. No available theory is consistent with the available data, and many approaches use ambiguous and subjective terms. Callway and Stone express the hope that the new psychotropic drugs can serve as a valuable class of independent variables in an integrated theory of behaviour.

It is to mention that the task of analyzing the specific pharmacological effects of a drug is confounded by the history, learned expectations, and social roles of the individuals involved. *Poffenberger (1942)* also discussed several major sources of error in drug investigations. He expressed serious concern about the "suggestibility of people who have a knowledge of the effects to be expected", the lack of control subjects, the difficulties in the selection of appropriate measures of drug effects.

It is necessary to mention that an analysis of psychopharmacology and personality takes stock of personality measurement in relation to drugs. It reports the rather meagre progress in psychopathology and deduces a static plateau in personality measurement "cushioned by factor analysis on the one hand and by psychodynamics on the other" *(Zubing & Katz, 1964)*.

One of the most important specific areas of treatment of hospitalized psychiatric patients, additional aspects of the effects of drugs become of interest to the social scientist. *Klerman (1961)* indicated that it is unfortunate for drug evaluation that the advent of the newer tranquillizing agents in the 1950s coincided with a wave of hospital reforms and innovations in the treatment of psychotic patients. This interaction is a complex one, and it is difficult to assess the effects of "Drugs" on hospital admission, readmission, and other rates.

In addition to affecting the individual patient or subject, the psychotropic drugs also affect the hospital milieu and functional organization. One of the most important scientists viz, *Elkes (1961)* has described this interaction as an age of revolutions, thus one is apt to get used to revolutions. In considering the impact of the pharmaco-therapies on the management of the psychoses in a mental hospital, one is apt to be reminded of the violent changes brought about in the past by the introduction of other somatic therapies, such as deep insulin coma, electroplexy, and the botomies. Each of these has wielded changes, based essentially upon relatively short-term results; only in recent years could these be viewed against the perspectives of long-term follow-up studies. The changes in management, and the attendant changes in attitude, however, have stayed and become cumulative. It is quite possible that a similar fate may befall the pharmacotherapies of mental disorder, though three important differences distinguish them from earlier treatments and encourage a more hopeful view. The first is the fact that these therapies can be graded and made individual in a way which was quite impossible with the less variable and massive procedures used in the past. Secondly, they can be used on a scale far larger than the earlier therapies. Thirdly, whereas in the past systematic studies of mode action followed essential empirical findings and measures, the empirical findings of the pharmacotherapies are being increasingly related to a growing body of modern theoretical neuropharmacology and neurochemistry. Theories are thus likely to keep abreast of clinical findings in a way never before witnessed in psychiatry, and are likely to make these ever more precise, discriminating and long-term.

The impact of the drug therapies on mental hospital population is essentially threefold. They have altered the immediate management and treatment of certain types of acutely disturbed psychotic patients; they have mobilized large chronic populations; hitherto secluded in the continued treatment units of the average mental hospital; and, in individual cases, have made possible measures of rehabilitation which would have been very difficult to achieve in their absence. Lastly, they have increased and made more urgent the contacts between the mental hospital and the community. In terms of all these effects the drugs are wielding profound changes in staff attitudes at all professional levels. The precise pattern of these changes at present is far from clear, and for the moment can only be discussed in the broadest terms.

One of the most important studies has been conducted by *Bullard, Hoffman, and Havens (1960)* who indicated that drugs may be more important than environment in producing changes in chronic patients. An excellent review of this problem by *Hordern and Hamilton (1963)* indicates its complexities and the lack of clarity regarding the contributions to patient response of drugs and special nondrug treatments and of staff and patient attitudes. It is unfortunate but true that the effects of the drug and/or environment found in any single study represent only a single case in the larger sense, since it is almost difficult at present to measure or even meaningfully hypothesize what aspects of the staff-patient-milieu-drug context are responsible for the effects produced.

6

ORGANIC ASPECTS OF DRUG ADDICTION

The term "drug addiction" has, generally, been applied in the criterion of habitual use of chemical agents (natural or synthetic) in spite of harmful consequences to the individual, society, or both. It is to point out that drug problem in India is not a new phenomenon, but the number of drug abusers has never been as high as it is today.

Numerous studies conducted in various parts of the country have reported an alarming increase in drug abuse. These have also revealed that the variety of drugs abused in the past have stretched out from cannabis and its preparations to other drugs such as opium, barbiturates, amphetamines, tranquillizers, LSD, mandrax, pathedine, acrophine, alcohol and heroin *(Singh & Lal, 1977; Sethi & Manchanda, 1977; Parameswaran & Rao, 1983; Nagaraja, 1985; Verma et al, 1978)*. There are large number of determinants and correlates of drug abuse such as personality, familial factors and social factors. Moreover, there are certain personality types which are more prone to drug abuse.

Youths in India have more recently been subjects for investigation of prevalence and pattern of drug abuse, as this fever is spreading like a wild fire amongst them. It is, undoubtedly a fact that drug habits of the younger generations have complex reasons and motivations for the deviant behaviour which had to be explored. In this chapter the term drug addiction has been used instead of drug abuse, drug habituation, or drug dependence, because the term drug addiction is more popular and widely used in daily life.

In part, harmful consequences may arise from the pharmacological and toxicological properties of the drug employed. These vary greatly, depending on the class of drug, the dose, and regularity and frequency of administration. Thus the toxic states induced by opioids which refers to all chemical substances with morphine like properties, including morphine itself are characterized by respiratory depression, stupor, or coma, barbiturates, certain nonbarbiturate sedatives, and alcohol can produce mental confusion, incoordination, and coma, cannabis products (marijuana, hashish), amphetamine and allied "stimulant amine," and cocaine, as well as a number of "Psychosomimetic" agents can give rise to psychoses of various sorts.

Repeated administration of opioids, barbiturates and allied drugs, or alcohol can give rise to a state of "Pharmacogenic" (or "Physical") dependence — a state such that always withdrawal of the drug is followed by physiological and psychological disturbances (abstinence syndromes), which are usually transient but may be fatal. These also differ, depending on the class of drug involved, for instance, predominantly autonomic disturbances in the case of opioids, and convulsions and delirium in the case of barbiturates, nonbarbiturate sedatives, or alcohol. Associated in varying degrees with the development of pharmacogenic dependence is the acquisition of "tolerance" — progressive decline in degree of effect produced by a given dose of the drug—which can be almost complete in opioid users but is achieved only partially by regular use of the barbiturate and allied drugs or alcohol. With the acquisition of tolerance, the user is impelled to increase progressively the dosage and/or frequency of administration in striving for the original effects, thereby incurring the risk of inducing toxic reactions and intensifying still further the degree of pharmacogenic dependence. It refers to a state that in itself has disastrous consequences for the psychological as well as the physical functioning of the user.

Social Consequences

It is to mention here that the harmful consequences of habitual drug use are social in nature. Even at subtoxic dose levels the effects of a given drug may impair the user's usefulness to the society in which he lives or may otherwise modify his behaviour in unacceptable ways. In addition, harmful consequences may result from the user's attendant neglect of the welfare of his dependents, through either indifference to them, diversion of income for purchase of drugs, or adverse effects on his own health caused by inattention to proper nutrition, hygiene, and treatment of disease. Since in most societies it has been found necessary to place legal restrictions on the manufacture and distribution of many drugs of abuse, criminalism constitutes anotherof the consequences of this practice.

Clinical Features of Addiction

The more commonly abused opioids include opium itself (containing 10 per cent morphine), morphine and certain of its derivatives, such as codeine, diacety morphine (heroin), dihydro-morphinone, dihydrohydroxycodeinone and a number of synthetic analgesics, such as meperidine (Pethidine, Demerol, Dolantin), Ketobemidone, methadone (Dolophine, Amidone), and *dextromoramide* (Palfium). Heroin is the most common opioid purveyed illicitly throughout the world, although opium is still widely used in the East Asia, it includes, India, China, and Japan. Important variations occur, depending upon the particular opioid and the mode of utilization (smoking, sniffing, ingestion, injection), but the effects of morphine under experimental conditions are quite illustrative of the specific patterns of chronic intoxication, tolerance, and pharmacogenic dependence that develop with repeated use of opioids in general.

It is to note that in nontolerant persons a single injection of a "therapeutic" dose of morphine (e.g., 15 milligrams) commonly produces a state of drowsiness from which the subject can be readily aroused. Pain, if present, is relieved and anxiety allayed. Particularly if injected intravenously, morphine may produce transient sensations in the abdomen that are sometimes described as akin to orgasms. Flushing of the skin and itching, as well as giddiness and vomiting are also common effects. Characteristically, the pupils are constricted, respiratory rate is depressed, the pulse is slowed and body temperature is lowered slightly. These effects which last four to six hours, may be evaluated as different ways by different subjects, depending upon circumstances, but even among future habitues the effects of the first injection of morphine (or heroin) are often judged as unpleasant. In continuation to this context, it is necessary to mention that muscular aches and twitches, abdominal cramps, vomiting and diarrohea, elevated blood pressure, insomnia, agitation, weight loss, spontaneous ejaculation in the male, and profuse menstrual bleeding in the female supervene later, developing maximally during the next two or three days and then subsiding gradually, although physiological normality may not be achieved for six months or longer. Such abstinence phenomena are quickly alleviated by injection of the accustomed dose of morphine (or on equivalent dose of another opioid), only to reappear some hours later. The untreated morphine abstinence syndrome is rarely fatal, except in patients with cardiac disease; active tuberculosis, or other weakening illnesses.

One of the most important diagonoses is pharmacogenic dependence on opioids that can be made in two ways: (a) by observation of the abstinence syndrome that ensues when the drug is withheld; and (b) by subcutaneous injection of specific morphine antagonist, such as nalorphine (3-15 mg. in divided doses). *Wikler (1962)* provides the details of treatment. Evaluation of the results obtained of treatment has been extremely difficult. The best evidence available, that of a large group of addicts returning to New York after treatment at the US Public Health Service Hospital in Lexington, Kentucky, indicates that over 90 per cent of the patients became addicted again, more than 90 per cent of these within six months after their discharge *(Hunt & Odoroff, 1962)*. In a study of four hundred opioid addicts (Caucasian) at the US Public Health Service Hospital, Lexington, *Brown (1940)* found them to be of average or slightly superior height and weight, with normal distribution of body build, although there was a trend toward the pyknic habitus. Electroencephalographic studies by *Andrews (1941)* on fifty addicts, (one year after drug withdrawal) revealed only that the groups differed from published data on "normals", in that among the addicts, individuals with occipital alpha indices either of 90-100 per cent or of 0-10 per cent were more common. In addition, morphine exerts depressant actions on the "skin-twitch" in the dog and the "tail-flick" in the rat, both of which have been used successfully in the screening of drugs for analgesic properties in man. In part, morphine affects these reflexes by a direct depressant action of spinal interneurons, but a major component of its action in the intact animal appears to be augmentation of supraspinal inhibition. From the neurophysiological standpoint, therefore, it would appear that morphine alters the "reaction" to noxious stimulation at several levels of the neuraxis rather than affecting propagation of impulses generated by such stimuli from the periphery to the cerebral cortex. As *Schaumann (1954)* has pointed out the analgesic action of morphine is but part of its "antiprotective" spectrum of effects, it is quite similar to the concept primary-need reducing, which has also been applied in this connection *(Wikler, 1952)*.

Much research has also been devoted to the problem of accounting for the selectivity that characterizes the sites of action of morphine in the central nervous system. In isolated smooth muscle preparations, morphine has been shown to reduce both the resting output acetylocholine and the output from postganglionic cholinergic nerve endings when they are stimulated, and to inhibit the release of sympathetic transmitter substance from postganglionic nerve endings in rats. Scientists have pointed out that single doses of morphine decrease the brain concentrations but repeated administration of morphine increases these concentrations. At the present time the precise manner in which these changes are related to pharmacogenic dependence is difficult to establish because of some differences in regard to details that depend on the species used and the techniques employed by the different investigators.

It is indeed, the phenomena of tolerance and pharmacogenic dependence appear to be due to changes at the cellular level, it is quite likely that certain features of the clinical opioid abstinence syndrome are modulated by "Counteradaptive" changes involving systems not directly affected, or only slightly affected, by this class of drugs.

7

PSYCHOLOGICAL ASPECTS OF DRUG ADDICTION

Drug addiction is one of the most burning problems of the whole world. There are many factors involved in drug abuse including biological, cultural and psychological factors. The concept of psychological proneness towards addiction refers to characteristics within the addicts which promote the use of drugs. Many studies, have demonstrated that some common personality traits are also prevalent among the drug abusers— they tend to score low on well being and self satisfaction; are inclined to be more non-confirming, more alone and isolated at home, less optimistic about vocational future and more disorganized under stress *(Gautam et al, 1991; Craig, 1979).*

It is necessary to stress light on some of the observations experienced by the present investigators, that is, drug addicts develop psychological abnormality against their own social group. Excessive abuse poses difficult problems for the drug addicts, their families, the production units to which the drug addicts are associated. It is true that drugs change the user's mood or perception to self and environment; drugs resolve their personal conflicts; drugs serve as the principle mode of recreation and relaxation; drugs provide relief from tension and physical exhaustion from prolonged work. There is growing evidence *(Brook, et al; 1980; Huba & Bentler, 1982)* for the notion that certain personality characteristics such as less sense of personal responsibility (e.g., lack of achievement motivation) and less sense of social responsibility (e.g., delinquency), enhance adolescent's proneness to drug abuse. An important study was conducted by *Hill, Haertzen, and Glaser (1960)* they concluded that narcotic addicts are often psychopathic, that hospitalized adolescent and adult addicts do not differ in their Minnesota Multiphasic Personality Inventory (MMPI) profiles, that great similarities exist between adolescent addicts and delinquent nonaddicts, and that psychopathology is an important etiological element in addiction.

However, very similar MMPI profiles have also been found by the group of investigators to characterize not only juvenile delinquents but also hospitalized chronic alcoholics *(Hill, Haertzen, and Davis, 1962)*. Speculating on the commonness of elevated scores for psychopathy in the MMPI among narcotic (opioid) and alcoholic subjects, *Hill (1962)* has suggested that the "social deviant" does not engage in the daily activities that are ordinarily reinforced by and satisfy the larger society. Counteranxieties and inhibitions that deter unusual behaviour in the mature adult do not do so in the social deviant. Thus, he is particularly vulnerable to short term satisfactions and can readily manipulate his personal affairs if drugs are available. The deviant who is immature and inadequate and is unable to solve problems of adult life independently may find temporary freedom from frustration and problems in alcohol or complete elimination of such problems in opiates. Moreover, other investigators have stressed "passive dependency" as a dominant trait among opioid addicts, and *Wikler and Rasor (1953)* have suggested that such individuals choose opioids for repeated use from among a number of other drugs, including alcohol, with which they have had experience precisely because the opioids facilitate their preferred mode of dealing with frustrating and anxiety-arousing situations - namely, by promoting "indifference", as would the use of alcohol. However, a major difficulty in relating personality characteristics found in opioid addicts to the addiction process is the paucity of suitable control data.

Hill et al (1962) while using the MMPI also compared 200 addicts with a group of 199 hospitalized alcoholics and group of 200 prisoners. Using a factor analytic technique, they identified three primary addict personality types: (i) the undifferentiated psychopath, (ii) the primary psychopath and (iii) the neurotic-psychopath.

In addition to the psychological aspects of drug addiction, it is necessary to mention that a high depression and psychopathic deviate (pd) score on the MMPI correlates with alcoholism and psychedelic flashbacks *(Heaton and Victor, 1976). Martin et al (1977)* have proposed that detoxified opium addicts and long abstaining chronic alcoholics have significantly elevated scores on the Psychopathic deviate (pd). Hypomania and depression scales of the MMPI literature demonstrated that addicts consistently have significantly elevated scores on the Psychopathic deviate (pd) scale.

As far as the psychological aspect is concerned, Indian studies report that drugs used in cities mainly by the middle and upper middle-classes, and by the young people from rich families *(Mohan, Thomas, Prabhu, 1978; Mohan and Arora, 1976; Varma et al; 1977).*

Veeraraghavan (1980) reported the main reasons for starting on a drug habit as "experimentation" or "curiosity" (61.6%) followed by "kicks" (36.1%) and "to get over problems regarding family, personal, failure, etc," (32.4%). Other reasons such as "to feel confident", "to remove boredom", "peer group pressures", "to intensify perception" and "aesthetic awareness", etc., were also advanced, but by a very few (range 3.14%) drug abusers. *Shanmugham (1981)* studied 212 male students chosen from the 1100 students as drug abusers in an earlier study *(Shanmugham, 1978).* Comparison of these to non drug users revealed that drug users were more extroverted, more neurotic, more psychotic and have more criminal propensity than non drug users.

In one of the most important studies, *Dhillon and Pawah (1981)* found that drug users felt emotionally very insecure as compared to their normal colleagues as they had strong feelings of rejection, isolation, of being unloved, anxiety, hostility, inferiority, helplessness and inadequacy. Thus studies revolve around the importance of psychological factors in drug addiction. It is to be pointed out that the "emotional" effects of morphine have been obtained by various scientists and others in a series of studies on "anxiety associated with the anticipation of pain" in postaddicts. It is necessary to point out that the effects of single doses of morphine on the so-called pain threshold are unpredictable *(Andrews, 1943; Denton & Beecher, 1949),* these investigators hypothesized that one important action of morphine in the production of analgesia is dissociation of "anxiety" from perception of the noxious stimulus. In agreement with this hypothesis, others found that morphine (15 mg) had no significant effect on the ability of postaddicts to estimate intensities of brief but painful electric shocks under "nonanxious" conditions;

under "anxious" conditions untreated subjects overestimated the intensity of such stimuli, whereas after injection of morphine the estimated and actual intensities of these stimuli did not differ significantly. Likewise, it has been reported that single doses of morphine (15 mg) significantly reduced the disruption of performance on a visual-manual reaction time test, produced by repeated self-inflicted electric shock penalties for slow reaction times - an action not shared by *pentobar bital (250 mg)*. Further evidence of the effectiveness of morphine in reducing "anxiety associated with anticipation of pain" was obtained by *Kornetsky (1954)* in a study on postaddicts, employing radiant heat stimuli instead of electric shocks. In addition to measurement of "stronger or weaker than standard" judgements of the noxious stimulus, several measures of "anticipation" were included, under both "anxious" and "non-anxious" conditions. It was found that morphine decreased significantly the number of "stronger" responses, as well as anticipatory psychogalvanic responses, only under "anxious" conditions. It is obviously clear from the mentioned studies that, atleast in postaddicts, single doses of morphine reduce responsivity to a variety of stimuli that have in common the property of producing "emotional" arousal.

Observations of the review of literature have clearly shown morphine produced euphoria would seem to be a decisive factor in reinforcing repeated use of this drug, the rapid development of tolerance to this effect results in marked changes in the behaviour of the addict. Thus, *Brown (1946),* in his long-term study on experimental readdiction in two subjects, noted that there was seldom a level of dosage that maintained satisfaction for a period longer than three weeks. There were no signs that morphine had increased the general sense of pleasantness, although there were short periods of euphoria. The general mood level during the period of addiction was one of unpleasantness. Similar observations were made by *Wikler (1952)* in a study on self-regulated experimental readdiction to morphine in a single postaddict. Over a period of three and a half months this subject progressively increased the size of each dose and the frequency of self-injection (intravenous) to a total daily dose level of about 1.350 mg of morphine taken in 12 divided doses throughout the day and night. Nevertheless, he was unable to regain the euphoric effects he had experienced initially after a single dose of 30 mg of morphine, and his prevailing mood was one of dejection, remorse, guilt, and anxiety, which were also reflected in his dream material.

Having scanned the review of literature regarding the organic and psychological aspects of drug addiction, it has been observed that the various roles assigned to pharmacogenic dependence which are still highly speculative and it seems to deserve intensive research, since one obvious fact about "drug-addiction" in general is that the drugs which create the most persistent degrees of "habitual use with harmful consequences" are precisely those which engender pharmacogenic dependence.

8

SOCIAL ASPECTS OF DRUG ADDICTION

Drug addiction is not a new phenomenon. In early ages, it was used in ritual ceremonies by having socially/religiously approved demands of the society. But its excessive use in the modern society is now leading to disastrous effects on mankind. It is now named as drug abuse. This is a social evil not only for Indian society but entire parts of the nations of the world.

The taking of drugs is a culturally patterned behaviour. Both the prevalence and the consequences of drug use in society depend as much upon social norms as upon physiological responses to drugs or general psychological characteristics of drug users. In the olden days, the use of drugs were varied such as, relief from pain, fatigue, or anxiety, the celebration of social solidarity, "kicks", and enhanced mystical experience. Beliefs about the effects of the substances used and the specific ends sought through such use are closely linked with more general cultural goals and orientations. A particular drug like marijuana (also called *hashish* and *bhang*) may be accepted as an appropriate adjunct to sociability in one society, used as an invaluable ingredient in religious contemplation in another, and banned by law as dangerous.

There is no evidence that addiction to drugs is favourably regarded in any society or culture, but the status accorded to the addict varies markedly. It is important to mention here that in the United States, it has been defined as a criminal, stereotyped and a "dopefied". In most of Europe, on the other hand, the addict is viewed as an unfortunate person whose problem is primarily psychological and medical. It is a matter of fact that great differences exist in cultural orientations to specific drugs or drug effects. We are, however, far from being able to explain them. Opium and Hashish have been widely used in Muslim society. The Quran in

Islamic Religion prescribes the use of substances that alter the state of consciousness. In traditional interpretations, it appears that Quran's injunction has been limited to alcohol.

To cite another example, a student of culture and personality has suggested that opium smoking was prevalent in China because it afforded a means of achieving the cultural goal of individual harmony with the environment. But opium smoking did not exist in China until it was introduced by European traders in the seventeenth century *(Sonnedecker, 1963)*. It is important to note that opium was subsequently forced upon the Chinese by the East India Company, despite protests by the Chinese government. An adequate understanding of drug use within a given culture requires a knowledge of historical facts that is rarely available.

In addition to above the beliefs and practices surrounding drug use reflect different perspectives and value orientations, the social correlates and the consequences of drug use will themselves vary substantially from one country to another and from time to time within any given country. Coffee and tobacco have, in various societies, been prescribed as debilitating or debauching. The smoking of tobacco was a crime punishable by death in Russia, Persia, Turkey, and parts of Germany *(Lewin, 1924)*. The term "drug" refers to a wide variety of chemical substances consumed by men/women, not merely to narcotics or "dangerous drugs". When applied to substances consumed outside the medical channels, however, "drug" tends to connote something negatively valued. Hence, we do not normally apply the term "drug habit" to the smoking of tobacco but we do to the smoking of marijuana, even though many more persons may be psychologically habituated to tobacco smoking than to marijuana.

It is very important to note that there is no single causal pattern that fits all narcotic addiction. In addition to the physiological and psychological dependence that itself becomes a driving factor, life stress, personal maladjustment, and sociocultural conditions enter into the total causal picture.

A majority of researchers, in the late 20th century, have isolated and studied receptor sites for narcotic drugs in the brain *(Pert & Snyder, 1973; Goldstein, et al, 1974)*. Such receptor sites are specific nerve cells into which given psychoactive drugs fit like a key into the proper lock. This interaction of drug and brain cell apparently results in the action of the drug and in the case of narcotic drugs leads to addiction.

It is to point out that addiction is generally associated with the relief of pain and with professional persons who have access to narcotic drugs. Many patients are given narcotic drugs, such as morphine to relieve pain during illness/surgery and or serious injury. The large majority of such patients never develop an addiction, and when their medication is discontinued, they do not again resort to the use of morphine. Those narcotic addicts who blame their addiction on the fact that they used drugs during an illness usually show personality deficiencies which predisposed them to the use of drugs - such as immaturity, low frustration tolerance, and the ability to distort and evade reality by way of a flight into drug-induced fantasy.

Addiction, indeed, is also associated with sociocultural aspects. The influence of sociocultural factors in drug dependence, including alcohol and opium addiction, is well depicted in the experience of the Meo, a tribal people who inhabit the mountains of several countries in Southest Asia *(Westermeyer, 1971)*. In our own society there are no opium dens, but there are so-called narcotic subcultures, in which it is easier for an addict to obtain drugs and to protect himself against the sanctions of society. It is generally seen that the majority of narcotic addicts do participate in the drug culture. It is important to mention here that the decision to join this culture has important implications for the future life of an addict and the people who are keen will center their activities around the role of a drug user. In short, their addiction becomes their way of life.

If we trace the historical background of social aspects of drug addiction, we find that through the Middle Ages, the primary use of opium was medical. The letters and records of European travellers in the orient during the Middle Ages occasionally refer to opium as a drug used by the people to overcome fatigue, but they do not mention chronic intoxication or indicate recognition of the phenomena of tolerance and dependency *(Sonnedecker, 1963)*.

The extent of drug use and drug addiction, historically or currently, is known only in very general terms. The use of opiates and of marijuana and the so-called "dangerous drugs" is devalued by the great mass of the population, not only in Western society but entire parts of the nations of the world.

In general, the prevailing sentiment toward drug use, even on the parts of residents of slum areas, is decidedly negative. It is generally seen that most children learn that heroin and marijuana are considered "bad" by most adults. In areas of highest drug use, however, rejection of the standards of conventional society, distrust of policemen, and relatively favourable attitudes towards drugs tend to be much more widely prevalent, even among a cross-section of school children, than in other areas of the city *(Chein et al, 1964)*.

Certain personality characteristics of narcotic addicts are markedly different from those of normal middle-class persons, and to a lesser degree they are different from those of non-addicted persons coming from the same social backgrounds as the addicts. One of the most important expression of the personality differences is in attitude. Addicts are characterized by attitudes of pessimism and futility on the one hand and of distrust and rejection of the standards and representatives of middle-class society on the other. The study of attitudes towards drug taking behaviour (use/abuse of psychoactive substances) is important for several reasons. Firstly, amongst the various student populations, it has been studied that attitude, belief and actual behaviour toward substance use are highly correlated *(Bhadra & Girija, 1981; Singh & Khan, 1981; Spencer & Navaratnam, 1980)*. Secondly, in the studies of *Abed & Neira Munoz, (1990); Geller et al (1989); Paton (1989). Chappel & Schnoll (1977)* pointed out that negative attitudes of medical students and physicians towards "alcoholics and drug addicts" may lead to under diagnosis and maltreatment in various medical settings. Finally, adverse attitudes of non-medical staff at various treatment facilities may also give rise to distress and discriminatory behaviour towards the patients of drug dependence *(Ball & Ross, 1991; Nurco et al, 1988)*.

As far as the attitudes towards drug taking behaviour is concerned, it is to highlight that the literature is relatively silent regarding the attitudes of the care givers and burden-sharers of the drug dependent person at home. In this regard, *Rao & Kuruvilla (1992)* studied and found that the families of substance abusers have to bear a major brunt of the problems posed by these persons and often find it difficult to cope with. Recently, *Basu, Malhotra,*

Verma and Malhotra (1977) have pointed out that their own attitudes towards drug taking behaviour would have an important bearing upon how they perceive and handle the difficulties at helm. It could only be guessed here that the Western researchers have neglected the study of this particular area because there the management is more institutional (drug abuse treatment centres, rehabilitation centres, half-way homes, methadone clinics, etc,) and less family-based (the drug dependent person there often coming from broken home, living alone or in ghetto subcultures).

Another major aspect of personality difference between the addict and the nonaddict is the low self-esteem and high degree of social immobilization of the narcotics user by virtue of anxiety. A major appeal to the opiates is that they should permit the constricted ego greater scope and freedom *(Chein, 1964)*. In one of the studies, conducted by *Clausen (1957)* who pointed out that the personality attributes appear to reflect aspects of the social environment in which the addict has been nurtured, particularly the devaluation and deprivation that are experienced by residents, especially minority group members, or urban slums. The same terms relating to personality characteristics have been used to describe slum dwellers elsewhere who were not involved in drug use. Within the areas of highest rates of drug use, users tend to come from families lacking a stable father figure, lacking warmth between parents, and characterized by vague or inconsistent standards. It is to point out here that these mentioned factors would tend to contribute to psychopathy in the child. Families with such characteristics are in part a product of migration to and life in the urban slum.

To the extent that narcotics or other drugs become the central preoccupation of an individual, as is true of an addict, that individual is likely to be an undependable employee. A substantial proportion of physician addicts are reported to have functioned adequately for long periods while addicted to narcotics, but the great majority of addicts are, at best, irregulary employed *(Schur, 1962)*. In addition, Schur stated that except for entertainers and physicians, the population from which addicts are drawn in the United States tends to be relatively disadvantaged in the job market. Since possession of a drug calls for more serious penalties than do most forms of these, there is little incentive for the active addict to work. Even in Britain, however, where addiction and drug possession are not defined as crimes, most addicts have unsatisfactory work records.

Moreover, in India and Sri Lanka the two nations in Asia with similar cultural and historical background, the story seems to be similar. It is reported that drug addiction/drug abuse is not a major public health problem in India as the use of drugs such as opium, cannabis, alcohol and tobacco was an integral part of the religious and social life of many communities *(Jiloha & Sahay, 1986).* Studies carried out in India around 1978 and 1979 reported that heroin was not a major drug of abuse at the time. Most commonly reported drugs of abuse were alcohol, cannabis and opium and these were reportedly being abused by addicts in their 40's and 50's *(Singh & Lal, 1978; Verma & Dang, 1978).* The figure changed in the early 80's with the alarming rise in the number of heroin addiction *(Adityanjee, 1984).*

Drug abuse has become a serious problem in Asian countries where specifically heroin abuse emerged as one of the devastating epidemics faced by Pakistan as *Najam (1997)* reported. In Pakistan, the researchers initiated drug abuse research soon after the drug ban was enforced in 1979. Prior to this ban, there were no legal restrictions on the use of different substances. Najam also reported that drugs were accepted as a part of Pakistani socio-cultural system. In fact, Bhang was (still is) ingested by the followers of various religious shrines during festivals similar cases being found in India. Like India, opium was traditionally used in Pakistan (and continues to be used) in medicines for diarrohea, cough, etc., prior to the 1979 ban, opium was available from authorized dealers and each user had to have a permit to buy only certain amount of opium from Government approved vendors. The ban appears in the same year as the Drug Control Arm of the United Nations, to assist the governments of the nations of the world by helping finance projects aimed at reducing the illicit supply of and demand for drugs. The United States is the primary contributor for this fund. In 1984, major donors for this fund agreed that development assistance to the narcotics growing regions should be linked to the governments commitment to control illicit drug production *(U.S. Report, 1986).*

Having discussed the psycho-social aspects of drug addiction, it has been observed that there is a need to pay much more attention for finding out the constraints of drug abuse and it should strictly be resolved by giving intervention strategies in an appropriate style. It is a fact that drug addiction is a social evil not only in India alone but entire parts of the world. Although, in various countries, the governments are also engaged in stopping drug abuse but parents, friends, teachers, doctors, learning centres, institutions, etc., may also play a vital role. This may be done by imparting educational programs related to drug abuse and its ill effects. These programmes may help if seen at an impressionable to age by the child.

9

SURVEY OF DRUG ABUSE IN INDIA

This chapter presents the studies and surveys conducted in India in the field of drug abuse done so far. There is evidence to show that in the age of *Mahabharat* and *Ramayana, 'Somras'* was drunk by kings and their courtiers the virtues of which ancient epics refer to. It was used in the worship of Lord Shiva. Certain preparation of cannabis like *bhang, charas* and *ganja* have long been used by priests and other religious personages as an aid to meditation in getting free from stress, depression and tension.

Opium was first used in India in the ninth century by the Arab traders. The use of opium and poppy pods increased during the Mughal period. Traditionally, it was used in medicines and as a sedative and pain killer. It was given in all kinds of ailments, like dysentery, diabetes, cough, etc. The use of cocaine for euphoric purposes, however, is not more than hundred years old in India *(Chopra, 1940, 1942)*.

Despite the fact that drug abuse is not new to India, yet there is ample evidence to point out that the use of mood-altering, habit-forming drugs and substances did not take up alarming proportions till recently *(Chopra & Chopra 1935, 1965; Govt. of India, 1977; Indian Council of Medical Research, 1977; Rao, 1962)*.

Available literature on drug addiction in India is either cross-sectional or retrospective and have generally been epidemiological and/or clinical in nature. *Chopra (1971)* stated that "from the paucity of literature on the subject, it appears that drug problems have not yet disturbed the Indian subcontinent. This is not so; maybe that the problem is not as serious as in other affluent countries, but it is spreading rapidly, particularly among the college and university students in large cities". The qualitative change in India's drug abuse scenario occurred after the sixties, when new varieties of narcotic drugs (heroin, smack, brown sugar, angel dust) and other psychotropic substances started surfacing on the scene *(Banerjee, 1963; Govt. of India, 1977; ICMR, 1977)*. Media reports, research reports and other publicity materials are witness that a non issue became a critical issue in India in the eighties. The college and school students, the unemployed youth, offsprings of broken families, and the blue collared workers were the most seriously affected. Cities like Delhi, Mumbai, Calcutta and Chennai have large numbers of addicts. Delhi alone is estimated to have more than a hundred thousand drug addicts, although, these numbers are at best intelligent guesses. It is quite possible that a much larger number may be existing unexposed, where the surveyors have not been able to reach *(Ahuja, 1986; Mohan, Sundram, Pal and Chawla, 1981; Khan and Krishna, 1984)*.

Chopra and Chopra (1965) have given a comprehensive and detailed account of the nature and extent of the drug use in India. They have also given the description of the economic, legal, social, religious, and cultural factors associated with the problems of drug abuse in India. They estimated that people with cannabis habit in India number over three million. They found that total consumption of cannabis in 1955 had gradually declined to 50 per cent of what it was in 1912-13. The figures remained constant during the years 1955-58, dropped again in 1959 and then rose once more in 1960.

There is also evidence to point out that drug-abuse is no longer limited to traditional user groups permeated to slum dwellers, industrial workers, and highly stress-prone persons belonging to the upper classes. Drug abuse has also afflicted a large number of young and adolescent persons, especially in the metropolitan areas *(Jiloha and Sahay, 1986; Jiloha and Manjal, 1985; Saxena and Mohan, 1984)*. Moreover, the rise of western style individualism and value system has not only eroded the traditional value system, but has not fully replaced it with an alternatively acceptable value system. In this transitional phase, it appears that more has been lost than gained *(Singh, 1975; Singh and Khan, 1981)*.

India is certainly facing a serious problem on account of drug-addiction. The youngsters from rich families usually become victims as they start taking drug as a fashion. The youngsters from the middle-class fall victims on 'learning', 'thrill', and 'enjoyment'. For the underprivileged students, to get into drug-abuse is triggered by a desire to escape the harsh and horrific realities of life. Various types of efforts have been made in this regard by numerous agencies from time to time to stop drug addiction. The government of India has already taken numerous steps by introducing an Act in 1985 which enhanced the punishment for drug addiction. Moreover, studies are being conducted to find out the causative factors of problems and its intervention strategies which are still in continuous process in the fight against the evil of drug addiction.

A nationwide survey on the prevalence of drugabuse has not yet been conducted but a number of studies and surveys available have been identified which highlight on the phenomenon *(Adityanjee, Mohan, and Saxena, 1984; Banerjee, 1989; Khan, 1985, 1989)*. In a study conducted by *Chopra (1940)*, taking into account the total quantity of the drug consumed, it deduced that one per cent of the total Indian population was addicted to cannabis. *Dube and Handa (1969)* reported that 0.77% out of 29,468 in general population habitually use alcohol.

Elnagar, Maitra and Rao (1971) conducted a study in a small community, with 1383 members from 184 families in West Bengal. They found that 1.3% of the rural population was addicted to alcohol and other drugs. In a survey conducted by *Dube and Handa (1971)* in and around Agra, 2% of the population studied was found to have problems of drug abuse. Nearly 60 per cent of them used alcohol, while the others were equally distributed between those who used cannabis on the one hand and those who used miscellaneous drugs on the other.

Thacore (1972) surveyed 497 families comprising a population of 2626. The results revealed that the rate of drug abuse was 18.55 / 1000 for taking alcohol, cannabis, tranquillizers and stimulants. In another survey conducted by *Deb and Jindal (1974)* in an area of 4 villages in Punjab it was found that 78.28% of the population used alcohol, whereas *Singh and Lal (1978)* observed that only 29.3% of the surveyed population used alcohol. *Singh (1978)* conducted another survey and found that alcohol use is confined almost entirely to males, and approximately half (49.6%) of all males of age 15 and above are alcohol users. The mean consumption per drinker, per year was estimated as 10,000 litres. *Dube (1972)* found that people in general were addicted to one drug or the other in 22.7 / 1000 cases in the city of Agra.

A report was submitted to the Ministry of Social Welfare, Government of India by *Mohan et al. (1977)* in which they pointed out that in the rural areas of Punjab, a large proportion of persons had never used or abused any drugs. Of the few who did, they used mainly alcohol, opium and cannabis. The proportion of regular users was very small and of addicts still smaller.

Clinical studies related to mental illness and drug abuse are many. Of these, a few *(Venkoba Rao, 1975; Bagadia et al., 1976)* have shown drug abuse in different context including self-medication for various disorders.

In one of the most important studies conducted by *Gupta, Narang, Gupta and Singh (1986),* they studied 250 rickshaw pullers and found that tobacco (92%) and alcohol (76%) were mainly used by them, whereas cannabis (16%) and opium (2.4%) were the substances most commonly used some time or the other by rickshaw pullers. *Sethi and Trivedi (1979)* in a field survey studied the population of 2415 individuals. Out of them only 2010 were above the age of 10 years who were considered in the study. 21.4% drug abusers were found in their study. Alcohol was found to be the commonest among drug abusers followed by cannabis. Maximum drug abusers (35.8%) were found in the age group of 35-44 years followed by the group with age 25-34 (16.5%) and 65 and above (15.8%). *Mohan et al. (1979)* found that 5.8% adult males out of 1031 respondents in rural Punjab consumed opium. *Varma et al. (1980)* studied and found that 23.7% were current users of alcohol, 16.0% admitted to having alcohol in the past but were not current users, and 60.3% had never consumed alcoholic beverages.

Recently, an important study was conducted by *Kumar (1994),* he pointed out that drug culture that was generally prevalent in college campuses till the early eighties has now shifted to the city slums in recent years. He also revealed that 50% of the drug addicts interviewed had sex almost daily, though only 23.3% of them were married and living with their partners, while 46.6% of the men confessed to patronizing prostitutes and many claimed to have casual sex partners, 60% of them were found never having used condoms. And that was because they were either unconcerned or ignorant about the way the HIV spreads. The study of Kumar also indicated that only 10% addicts earned Rs 12000 and above while

53.3% were totally dependent on others, 23.3% of them were daily wage earners and the rest did odd jobs.

In addition to the above surveys on drug abuse in general, studies in India have focussed exclusively on student population. For example, the studies of *Banerjee (1963), Veeraraghavan (1972), Chitnis (1974), Mohan (1976), Varma et al. (1977)* have surveyed exclusively the student population. These studies by and large have brought out the fact that drug abuse among students was present in a very small percentage and that too was related mainly to socially acceptable drugs like tobacco, alcohol and pain killers. The prevalence rate for tobacco was highest in Chennai (15.2%) and lowest in Hyderabad (6.3%). The prevalence rate for alcohol was highest in Mumbai (15.1%) and lowest in Hyderabad (9%). The prevalance rate for pain killers was highest in Delhi (20.9%) and lowest in Chennai (1.2%). As far as tranquillizers are concerned, the highest prevalence rate of tranquillizers in Delhi was 2.9% and lowest in Mumbai and Chennai, i.e. 1.01%. The use of cannabis was highest in Varanasi (10.9%) and the use of cocaine and LSD was negligible in all the centres.

Singh (1979) studied drug abuse among medical students and found that a number of social and developmental factors were closely linked to drug abuse and that one could predict the academic performance of students, their characteristics of lying, cheating and promiscuity by merely knowing their drug taking status. *Varma and Dang (1979)* also studied non-medical use of drugs amongst school and college students and found that alcohol was number one drug used by students (21.57%) and tobacco (12.1%) in that order which was followed by amphetamines (4.0%), tranquillizers (3.5%), sedatives (3.2%), cannabis (3.0%) and opium (2.1%) were the substances most commonly used some time or the other by students. *Mohan and Arora (1976)* reported a study on the students from various colleges of Delhi University and found a prevalence rate of drug-addiction i.e. 24.7%. Tobacco was the highest (19.76%) followed by alcohol (18.58%), tranquillizers (6.58%), amphetamines (4.23%), barbiturates (1.17%). Moreover, *Dube (1972)* reported 5% of all students in one university to be regular cannabis users. Whereas, *Bannerjee (1963)* in a study of 1,132 students in Calcutta University reported prevalence rate of drug abuse, i.e. tobacco (26%) and amphetamines (11.4%).

Ponundurai et al. (1984) in their study to assess factors pertaining to alcohol and drug abuse among internees with the help of youth survey questionnaire developed by WHO, found that 22.67% per cent of males indulged in alcohol abuse at least once a month. Correspondingly, cannabis was the most commonly abused drug by 9.33% of the male internees followed by sedatives and tranquillizers. The common causes advanced for such drug abuse were: to be sociable, for enjoyment, curiosity, relief from psychological stress, etc. Friends had been the main source of introducing the drug such as marijuana and amphetamines. In a survey of heroin dependence in New Delhi, *Adityanjee et al (1984)* pointed out, a sudden rise of heroin dependence amongst the young educated males which was attributed to easy availability of these drugs in the recent years and a marked decrease in their cost. It is to be pointed out that student population has been the focus of many researchers, since this group was considered as a high risk group. In this connection *Dayal (1972)* conducted a study on a population of 5,000 students of Delhi University, and found that almost 4% students had drug dependence of one type or the other. *Chitnis (1974)* reported a prevalence of 19.7% among students of Bombay University. Cannabis was the most commonly used drug in this area. *Varma et al. (1977)* reported a prevalence rate of 18.87% among college students of Chandigarh. *Dube et al. (1977)* have reported 9.68% of medical and 5.38% of non-medical students of Agra as regular drug abusers. *Dube (1977)* has already analysed the drug abuse problem among 1061 students of Agricultural University in Punjab, and reported overall prevalence rate of 29.6 per cent. In the same year *Sethi and Manchanda (1977)* reported a 48.1 per cent prevalence rate of drug abuse among Lucknow University students.

Mohan et al. (1977) studied the prevalence rate and pattern of drug abuse among students of Delhi University. They defined drug-abuse as "non-medical use of drugs"; dependence as "a state of inability to do without drugs, arising from repeated administration of drugs, on a periodic or continuous basis"; experimental user as "using one or more substances once a month or less often"; regular user as "those taking one or more drugs at least once a week or more often"; and addiction as "inability to stay without using one or more drugs". In this study 576 students were covered by them. They showed the prevalence of drug abuse as 32.2 per cent. The prevalence was higher among males and among students staying in hostels. Experimentation was the major cause of drug abuse. LSD, opium and cocaine were hardly used in a regular way. Tobacco and alcohol were the most frequently used drugs, followed by cannabis, amphetamines, barbiturates, anti-depressants and tranquillizers. *Chakraborty et al. (1980)* studied drug abuse among medical students of Calcutta University. The study revealed that 44.9 per cent of the students were using dependence producing drugs. Majority of them were using it experimentally. Only 3.2% were regular users. The drugs most commonly used were alcohol, cannabis and barbiturates. Curiosity was the commonest reason for drug abuse. Only 17 per cent of the first year students were drug abusers while almost 50 per cent of the final year students were taking drugs.

Singh and Singh (1980) conducted a study among 520 students of Punjab University in order to determine the extent of drug abuse among them, its frequency, age time of onset and the various social causative factors of drug abuse. The drugs included in the study were alcohol, tobacco, cannabis, amphetamines, tranquillizers, sedatives and opium. They found that alcohol was the most commonly used drug, followed by tobacco. Drug abuse was found more prevalent among older age group students, males, and among those who were living away from home and *Broota and Singh (1986)* also studied 120 students for assessing the adjustment problems and socio-personal variables in drug abuse. They found that prolonged usage of drug was associated with psychological maladjustment.

Recently, *Ahmad et al. (1995)* studied the prevalence of drug-abuse among Aligarh Muslim University students. In their study, out of 260 students, 7.7% students admitted to have taken hard drugs like alcohol (3.1%), cannabis (0.8%), sedatives (0.8%) and tranquillizers (3.1%). It is important to mention that *Ahmad et al. (1995)* reported the significance of difference between male and female students, so far as addiction of hard drugs is concerned. They also interestingly reported that out of the total sample (N=260), 69 students (Male=45 and Female=24) i.e. 26.5% were found to have taken soft drugs which included *bidi*/cigarette and *Hukka* or hubble-bubble (tobacco).

Efforts are being continued by researchers to find out the problem of drug abuse. The prevalence rates reported by the researchers vary, the reason being that different studies have taken different definitions of the problem. Many of the studies have been conducted on a small population as well Thus the available survey of literature on drug-abuse particularly on the population of students suggests that studies should be conducted on a larger and varied sample. On the basis of generalizations emanating from the study, the overall problems of drug abuse can be chalked out. Finally appropriate intervention strategies might be given to tackle the problem.

10

THE PRESENT STUDY

This section covers the aims and objectives of the present investigation. Previous chapters have already covered the general introduction of drug abuse, types of drugs and their uses and the survey of literature on drug abuse especially in the Indian context.

The present study was aimed at analysing the prevalence rate of drug abuse among Delhi University students. The study was undertaken to understand the psycho-social concomitants. There are students who opt for drugs and students who don't, having a relatively similar sociocultural pressure and the knowledge of availability of such drugs. The psychological and social variables responsible for drug abuse are thus, a concern of this study.

It is believed that there are many reasons to becoming an intoxicant/drug user. Drug abuse behaviour is a symptom of personality problems which may be either psychological, social or medical.

Both sociologists and psychologists have given various explanations for drug abuse as a symptom of the problem. But definite etiology is still not known which could specifically pinpoint the cause of this problem. The assumptions which are widely accepted are certain background variables such as types of family, parents' occupation and family income. So, it was planned to study the prevalence of drug abuse among students in relation to these variables in this survey. Drug abuse by youth especially by students is a serious problem for the country. *Ray (1972)* pointed out that those users who centre their life, for one reason or another, around the use of these drugs become dropouts and fail to make any contribution to the present society.

Drug related problems crop up in many areas of life. The physical and mental health, work life, marital and family relations seem to be greatly affected by drug abuse. In the present study, therefore, variables like mental health and physical health have also been incorporated.

The use of drugs also has an important interrelationship with social trends in the culture. Hence, concern should not only be with medical effects of the drug or with the possible consequences of drug use but with the implications the extensive use of drugs may have on the society as a whole. For this reason various types of background variables of drug-abusers and non-abusers were taken for the accuracy and efficacy of the present study. Thus, the investigation is an attempt to study the prevalence rate of drug abuse among students who are studying in Delhi University. There are various types of drugs such as cigarette/*bidi* or *hukka*, smack, alcohol, opium, heroin, cannabis, tranquillizers, barbiturates, amphetamines and sedatives and the survey included all these types of drugs. Moreover, to compare the non-abuser group with that of user group, various types of psycho-social variables were also taken.

To estimate the prevalence rate of drug abuse among students, a questionnaire on the lines of World Health Organization (WHO) for drug use prevalence survey was prepared. Information regarding the drug abuse history and other variables was collected by.tapping the biographical information blank (BIB) attached with the questionnaire. Data were collected from the student populations individually after establishing good rapport with the subjects.

Objectives of the Study

Main objectives

The main objectives of the study were aimed at studying the prevalence rate of drug abuse among the different professionals and non-professional groups of Delhi University students. 'General group' included, B.A., B.Sc, B.Com, M.A., M.Sc., M.Com and research scholars. Moreover, medical students, engineering students, and nursing students were also taken in the study. Each student was identified and records were maintained in relation to family income, type of family and parents' occupation. Physical and mental health of the students were also judged.

Hypothesis

On the basis of the objectives of the present study, the following three hypotheses were formulated :

(i) Drug abusers in each category of students differ in terms of types of drugs and strength of their uses.

(ii) Drug abusers and non-abusers in each category differ in terms of their physical and mental health.

(iii) Drug abusers and non-abusers differ in terms of various background variables, viz., types of family, parents' occupation and family income.

11

METHODOLOGY

The present endeavour is intended to study the prevalence of drug abuse among Delhi University students and moreover, it was to find out the comparison between abusers and non-abusers group in terms of their psycho-social concomitants. For any kind of research, its methodology plays an important role in carrying out the study systematically. *Edwards (1971)* believed that "in research we do not haphazardly make observations of any and all kinds, but rather our attention is directed towards those observations that we believe to be relevant to the questions we have previously formulated. The objective of research, as recognized by all sciences, is to use observation as a basis for answering questions of interest". Edward's contention reflects the point that researches should be well-planned and must be carried out using sound means and techniques for investigation.

Researches always provide some knowledge and "the knowledge is inherently a social commodity to be shared and used" *(Runkel & McGrath, 1972)*. This idea reveals the fact as pointed out by *Mohsin (1984)* that if the social commodity, and 'knowledge' is being used by others then it should be acceptable to them and the basis for knowledge, in fact, should be known together with the procedure adopted for arriving at it.

In view of the above descriptions it has been found that methodology is the key element in carrying out any kind of research activity. In all researches, the objectivity of the investigation is contingent upon the accuracy of research methodology. The choice of methodology for research is determined by nature of the problem because every specific research demands a particular process and operations to be undertaken for carrying out investigations. After careful formulation of the problem, the thing which is of foremost importance is the design of the research.

Research design refers to a series of stipulated scientific procedures which have their importance in carrying out the research and to draw unbiased inferences. According to *Lindquist (1956)* who pointed out that "research design is the plan, structure and strategy of investigation conceived so as to obtain answer to research question and to control variance". *Mohsin (1984)* has already pointed out that "research design depicts the plan which states the relation between observed facts and events on the basis of which conclusion, a built-in system of check against all factors that might affect the validity of the research outcome". Therefore, it is to be said that the choice of appropriate design depends upon the special characteristics and availability of the sample, nature of measuring instruments and restraints regarding the manipulation of variables being studied. Our understanding of research design helps in carrying out the investigation to fulfil ultimate objectives with utmost objectivity.

The aim of the present study being to investigate the "prevalence rate of drug abuse among Delhi University students, and to study the comparison between drug abusers and non-abusers in terms of their psycho-social concomitants" itself speaks that the present work is a field study and in this condition the researcher has to go to study in real life situations. Therefore, such study is of greater value from the practical point of view.

The nature of the proposed research plan being a field study, the present investigator had chosen the group of students from various professional and non-professional colleges and various departments of Delhi University where they were engaged in studying and were residing in different hostels of Delhi University and other private places as well.

It is important to mention here that to seek information on the use of drugs from students is an extremely difficult task. The main problem is identifying those who take drugs because the sale and possession of many of the addictive drugs are prohibited by law. The use of drugs is also looked upon as in the nature of a serious aberration. It is, therefore, understandable that those who take drugs, specially students, are extremely secretive and are not prepared to part with any information in regard to this matter. The fact that intimate social contacts of those who use drugs are generally limited to other drug users makes it additionally difficult to conduct a study which will produce any significant information in regard to the use of drugs.

In view of the above situation and condition of the limited resources available, it was decided that the present study should be exploratory in nature. It should be entirely based on larger and varied samples so that prevalence rate of drug abuse could be estimated from the obtained information through survey questionnaire of drug abuse. However, the study does give reasonably reliable informations covering socio-economic background and facts pertaining to drug use in respect of students who served as respondents for this study.

Having discussed the methodology, research design and the nature of the proposed research study pertaining to the sample, the other steps which had been taken are as follows:

Sample

A sample may be referred to a small group representing the entire population. A population is a set of all possible observations or measurements of some common characteristics about which the researchers are interested in giving information. A sample is a part of this set. A large sample is to be prefered than a smaller one *(Fisher, 1950)* for obtaining reliable results.

The sample of this study consisted of students who are engaged in studying in different professional and non-professional colleges of Delhi University and the various departements of University as well.

The sample of the present study consisted of 1600 students taken from the various hostels of Delhi University and various parts of Delhi where they were residing on their own expense.

The category wise break-up of the total sample has been given in Table 11.1 as follows :

TABLE 11.1

Break-up Of The Total Sample Among The Delhi University Students

Sample (Category)	*N (Students)*	*Age (Range)*	*Mid-point of Age*
General	770	18 - 30	24
Medical	325	17 - 29	23
Engineering	375	19 - 27	23
Nursing	130	17 - 25	21
Total	1600		22.75

Description of Sample

It is essential to mention that the "general group" of students consisted of 770. These samples were drawn mainly from the postgraduate and undergraduate students. The students were engaged in studying and having different backgrounds from the disciplines of arts, social sciences, commerce, and natural science. They were also recorded to have subjects like, political science, sociology, psychology, history, Hindi, Urdu, chemistry, physics, mathematics, zoology, botany and commerce. It is also important to mention that an effort was also made to collect the information regarding the drug abuse from the research scholars of Delhi University. As a result of this some of the research scholars from various disciplines were also contacted to gather information regarding the drug abuse. In this group, the subjects' age ranged from 18-30 years.

Similarly, the group of medical students consisted of 325. These students were mainly drawn from the various departments of medical colleges. Generally, the subjects were having the idea about the usage of drug and their consequences and did not hesitate to fill up the questionnaire. In this group the subjects' age ranged from 17-29 years.

The group from engineering colleges consisted of 375 students. These students were contacted from the departments, hostels and the private places where they were residing. In this group students were having different branches of disciplines like civil, mechanical, electrical, etc. The subjects' age ranged from 19-27 years.

Lastly, the nursing group consisted of only 130 students. This group was mainly taken either from their respective study centre or from their hostels. The sample's age ranged from 17-25 years

Description of Tools Used

There are various methods to acquire information regarding a research problem. Human behaviour is a very complicated phenomenon which varies from person to person and from mood to mood in different sociocultural milieu. There is no single psychological test which can tell about all aspects of behaviour. Therefore, different tests are developed for different specific purposes. Questionnaire method has been considered as a convenient and favoured method to gather data regarding the numerous aspects of the problem.

As far as the proposed problem entitled "Prevalence of Drug-abuse among Delhi University Students : A Study of some Psycho-social Concomitants" is concerned, a questionnaire method was employed to gather information regarding prevalence of drug abuse.

To find out the prevalence rate of drug abuse among Delhi Universtiy students, a questionnaire on the lines of World Health Organization for drug use prevalence was prepared. Information on drug use included types of drugs used such as *bidi*/cigarette/or *hukka,* smack, alcohol, opium, heroin, cannabis, tranquillizers, amphetamines, barbiturates, and sedatives, frequency and duration of use, reasons for starting drugs, sources of procurements and the reasons for drug usage. Respondents were also asked places where drugs are used frequently. Moreover, the idea of the respondents, on the question like what is the meaning of drug usage, were also recorded. The schedule included questions seeking to ascertain from the respondents' knowledge about the consequences of drug usage and their effects. They were also asked to express their views on whether it is possible to stop drug supply for drug addicts and moreover, who can help to stop taking of drugs Respondents were also asked to furnish the questions regarding their mental and physical health.

The information schedule sought information on the personal and family background of the respondents. This included age, sex, marital status, family income, educational and other achievements. It also included information regarding the history of drug addicts like addiction among parents, family members and friends. Those who admit the drug use by family members themselves were requested to give a detailed information asked in the questionnaire.

Procedure

To collect the data, the printed questionnaires were given individually to each student after establishing proper rapport with the students in general and their sources in particular. Students were requested to answer each question freely without any hesitation and they were assured that their information will be kept strictly confidential.

Data were obtained from 1625 students. Finally, however, data of 1600 students were analysed. The break-up of the total sample has already been mentioned in Table 11.1.

After tabulating the responses obtained from each group, the frequency was counted. Students were identified as the drug abusers and non-abusers for further analysis in terms of psycho-social concomitants.

12

RESULTS

The present study was aimed at investigating the prevalence rate of drug abuse among Delhi University students and also to make a comparison between drug users and non-users of each group of students (General, Medical, Engineering and Nursing) in relation to some psycho-social concomitants. To meet the requirements of the proposed research endeavour each group of drug abusers were identified by counting the frequencies of intake and types of drugs used by them. The details of the different types of used drugs and their psycho-social concomitants of each group will be highlighted along with the description of results under various tables.

The results of the investigation on "Prevalence of Drug-Abuse among Delhi University Students : A study of some Psycho-social concomitants" have been described in detail. First of all, the results of the total sample will be taken into consideration and thereafter sub-samplewise description of results will be made.

Table 12.1 clearly describes the prevalence rate of drug-abuse from the total sample on different soft and hard drugs. The Table shows that cigarette, *bidi* (tobacco) have a very high degree of prevalence rate among both professional and non-professional groups of students as well as among the sample group as a whole as prevalence percentage rate ranges from 17.85% (medical group) to 22.73% (general group). In the light of the result it can be said that tobacco chewing and smoking is not being considered now as drug or something forbidden in the society. But other drugs are not very much prevalent irrespective of the professional and non-professional group as their prevalence percentage rate is very low which is shown very clearly in the table (Table 12.1). It is imperative to mention here that nursing group of students have not provided

TABLE 12.1

Overall Picture of Prevalence Rate of Drug-Abuse on Different Types of Drugs Among Students

Drugs	*General N=770*	*Medical N=325*	*Engineering N=375*	*Nursing N=130*	*Total N=1600*
Cigarette/*Bidi* (Tobacco)	175 (22.73%)	58 (17.85%)	80 (21.33%)	-	313 (19.56%)
Alcohol	68 (08.83%)	44 (13.54%)	75 (20.00%)	-	187 (11.69%)
Opiates	3 (00.39%)	3 (00.92%)	5 (01.33%)	-	11 (00.69%)
Cannabis	8 (01.04%)	(00.00%)	3 (00.80%)	-	11 (00.69%)
Tranquillizers	22 (02.86%)	8 (02.46%)	8 (02.13%)	-	38 (02.38%)
Amphetamines	4 (00.52%)	5 (01.54%)	5 (01.33%)	-	14 (00.88%)
Opium	0 (00.00%)	0 (00.00%)	0 (00.00%)	-	0 (00.00%)
Heroin	0 (00.00%)	0 (00.00%)	0 (00.00%)	-	0 (00.00%)
Barbiturates	4 (00.52%)	0 (00.00%)	2 (00.53%)	-	6 (00.38%)
Sedatives	2 (00.26%)	2 (00.62%)	2 (00.53%)	-	6 (00.38%)
Cigarette and alcohol	26 (03.38%)	0 (00.00%)	0 (00.00%)	-	26 (01.63%)
Cigarette and cannabis	5 (00.65%)	0 (00.00%)	0 (00.00%)	-	5 (00.31%)
Cigarette and tranquillizers	1 (00.13%)	0 (00.00%)	0 (00.00%)	-	1 (00.063%)
Cigarette and amphetamine	1 (00.13%)	0 (00.00%)	0 (00.00%)	-	1 (00.063%)
Cigarette, alcohol and cannabis	1 (00.13%)	0 (00.00%)	0 (00.00%)	-	1 (00.063%)
Total drug-users	320 (41.56%)	120 (36.92%)	180 (48.00%)	-	620 (38.75%)

any clue of taking any sort of either soft drug or hard drug, hence, their percentage rate comes to absolute zero.

TABLE 12.2

Frequency And Percentage of Cases Among Different Group of Students on Hard and Soft-Drugs.

Group	*N*	*Hard drug users*	*Soft drug users*	*Non users*
General	770	145 (18.83%)	175 (22.73%)	450 (58.44%)
Medical	325	62 (19.08%)	58 (17.85%)	205 (63.08%)
Engineering	375	100 (26.67%)	80(21.33%)	195 (52.00%)
Nursing	130	-	-	130 (100.00%)
Total	1600	307 (19.19%)	313 (19.56%)	980 (61.25%)

Table 12.2 describes the prevalence rate of the use of hard and soft drugs among different groups of students as well as in the total sample. It is clear from the table that percentage rate of using soft and hard drugs are almost similar among all the groups of students with the variation of negligible percentage that may evoke any significant of difference statistically. It is important to point out that whatever the percentage rate of drug addicts concerned, but the frequency of the use of hard drug is much more in medical and engineering groups compared to soft drug users which seems to be a horrible sign for society because it may lead to various psycho-social problems.

TABLE 12.3

Percentage Rate of Different Types of Drugs Used By Different Groups of Drug-Abuser Students (Total Drug Abuser N=620 Out of 1600 Students)

Drugs	*General N=320*	*Medical N=120*	*Engineering N=180*	*Total N=620*
Cigarette/*Bidi* (tobacco)	175 (54.69%)	58(48.33%)	80(44.44%)	313(50.48%)
Alcohol	68 (21.25%)	44(36.67%)	75(41.67%)	187 (30.16%)
Opiates	3(00.94%)	3(02.50%)	5(02.78%)	11(01.77%)
Cannabis	8(02.50%)	-	3(01.67%)	11(01.77%)
Tranquillizers	22(06.88%)	8(06.67%)	8(04.44%)	38(06.13%)
Amphetamines	4(01.25%)	5(04.17%)	5(02.78%)	14(02.26%)
Opium	—	—	—	—
Heroin	—	—	—	—

Barbiturates	4(01.25%)	—	2(01.11%)	6(00.97%)
Sedatives	2(00.63%)	2(01.67%)	2(01.11%)	6(00.97%)
Cigarette and alcohol	26(08.13%)	—	—	26(04.19%)
Cigarette and cannabis	5(01.56%)	—	—	5(00.81%)
Cigarette and tranquillizers	1(00.31%)	—	—	1(00.16%)
Cigarette and amphetamines	1(00.31%)	—	—	1(00.16%)
Cigarette, alcohol & cannabis	1(00.31%)	—	—	1(00.16%)

Table 12.3 shows the different types of drugs which were used by different groups of students. Each group of students along with the total sample of this table will be presented one by one.

General group consisted of 770 students. Out of 770 students, 320 (41.56%) students of general group reported to have taken drugs including soft drugs like cigarette/*bidi* (tobacco). It is important to mention here that hard drugs like alcohol (21.25%), opiates (.94%), cannabis (2.5%), tranquillizers (6.88%), amphetamine (1.25%), barbiturate (1.25%), sedatives (.63%) taken by them were reported. In this group of students, few students were found to have taken soft drugs along with the hard drugs: Cigarette followed by alcohol (8.13%); cigarette followed by cannabis (1.56%); cigarette followed by tranquillizers (.31%); cigarette followed by amphetamine (.31%); cigarette/Alcohol followed by cannabis (.31%) respectively (Table 12.3).

From the Table 12.2, it could be seen that medical group consisted of 325 students. Out of these 120(36.92%) students are found to be drug users. 58(48.33%) students admitted to the habit of tobacco chewing and cigarette smoking, whereas, 36.67% of students are found to be using alcohol in which most of them reported that alcohol was used occasionally. Very few drugs were reported to have been taken by them like tranquillizers (6.67%), amphetamines (4.17%), and sedatives (1.67%). No other drugs were reported by this group as shown in Table 12.3.

It is also observed from the Table 12.2 that engineering group consisted of 375 students. Out of these, 180(48%) students are found to have taken drugs which included tobacco (44.44%) and alcohol (41.67%). It is clear from the Table that only few students

TABLE 12.4

Frequency and Percentage of Cases Among Drug Abusers of Hard Drug and Soft Drug (Total Drug Abusers N = 620 Out of 1600 Students)

Groups	*N*	*Hard Drug Users*	*Soft Drug Users*
General	320	145 (45.31%)	175 (54.69%)
Medical	120	62 (51.67%)	58 (48.33%)
Engineering	180	100 (55.56%)	80 (44.44%)
Total	620	307 (49.52%)	313 (50.48%)

TABLE 12.5

Frequency and Percentage of Drug Users and Non-users' Among Different Group of Students

Groups	*No. of Students*	*Drug Users*	*Non-Users*
General	770	320 (41.56%)	450 (58.44%)
Medical	325	120 (36.92%)	205 (63.08%)
Engineering	375	180 (48.00%)	195 (52.00%)
Nursing	130	-	130 (100.00%)
Total	1600	620 (38.75%)	980 (61.25)

were reported to have taken hard drugs, i.e. opiates (2.78%), cannabis (1.67%), tranquillizers (4.4%), amphetamines (2.78%), barbiturates (1.1%) and sedatives (1.11%).

The sample survey of the nursing group consisted of 130 students, of which none reported to have used drugs.

Table 12.4 depicts at a glance the total sample survey consisting of 1600 students. Out of these, 620 (38.75%) of the students are found to have taken drugs covering all the categories mentioned except opium, heroin and smack which were not used at all. The proposed hypothesis is that drug abusers of each group differ in terms of the types of drugs and strength of their use to be accepted.

In the present study, two types of drugs were taken—soft drugs and hard drugs. Soft drugs, which include *bidi* / cigarette and *hukka*. These are, in view of the present investigation, called as tobacco chewing or smoking. On the other hand, the drugs like alcohol, cannabis, tranquillizers, amphetamines, opium, heroin, barbiturates, etc., are called hard drugs.

Table 12.4 highlights the frequency and percentage of cases among abusers of hard drugs and soft drugs. It can be observed from the Table that 307 students out of 620 drug abusers are found to have taken hard drugs and the percentage of the hard drug users is 49.52% as given in Table 12.4. Out of total hard drug users, 45.31% of general group, 51.67% of medical group, 55.56% of engineering group are reported to have taken hard drugs. On the other hand 54.69% of general group, 48.33% of medical group and 44.44% of engineering group are found to have taken soft drugs. At a glance, only 313 (50.48%) of the students out of 620 drug abusers were reported to be in the habit of tobacco. It is important to note that only the nursing group of students did not report either using hard drugs or soft drugs.

Table 12.5 indicates the strength of drug users and non-users of each group. It could be seen from the Table that general group of students consisted of 770 students. Out of these 320 (41.56%) students are found to be drug users whereas, 450(58.44%) students are reported to be non-users. Similarly, 120(36.92%) of medical students are found to be drug users and 205(63.08%) of students are reported to be non-users; whereas, 180(48%) of engineering students have been found to be drug users and 195(52%) of this group were reported non-users. It is important to mention here that only the nursing group did not report the use of any drugs or substances. Therefore, this group is considered 100% non-users. The Table clearly shows that 620(38.75%) students out of the total sample (N =1600) are found to have taken drugs hence it is to be called as drug users group. On the other hand 980(61.25%) students out of total sample were recognized as non-users. The proposed hypothesis, i.e. the strength of drug users of each group will differ from each group of non-users, stands to be accepted. Moreover, the comparison between drug abusers and non-abusers of each group could also be seen from the Table 12.5.

Table 12.6 highlights the percentage of cases in respect of various important and relevant background variables of drug-users group. Each group of the results will be highlighted one by one.

TABLE 12.6

Percentage of Cases in Respect of Various Backgrourd Variables of Drug-Users Group

Variables	*General N=320*	*Medical N=120*	*Engineering N=180*	*Nursing N=130*	*Total N=620*
Type of Family					
Nuclear	193(60.31%)	82(68.33%)	122(68.78%)	—	397(64.03%)
Joint	127(39.69%)	38(31.67%)	58(32.22%)	—	226(35.97%)
Father's Occupation					
Govt. Service	131(40.94%)	44(36.67%)	69(38.33%)	—	244(39.35%)
Pvt. Service	83(25.94%)	36(30.00%)	64(35.56%)	—	183(29.52%)
Business	106(33.13%)	0(33.33%)	7(26.11%)	—	193(31.13%)
Family Income					
0 - 2000	26(08.13%)	18(15.00%)	23(12.78%)	—	67(10.81%)
2000 - 4000	27(08.44%)	19(15.83%)	24(13.33%)	—	70(11.29%)
4000 - 6000	45(14.06%)	23(19.17%)	43(23.89%)	—	111(17.90%)
6000 - 8000	86(26.88%)	35(29.17%)	63(35.00%)	-	184(29.68%)
8000 - 10000	74(23.13%)	19(15.83%)	15(08.33%)	—	108(17.42%)
10000 - 12000	21(06.56%)	04(03.33%)	04(02.22%)	—	29(04.68%)
12000 - 14000	4(01.25%)	—	1(00.56%)	—	05(00.81%)
14000 - 16000	17(05.31%	—	03(01.67%)	—	20(03.23%)
16000 - 18000	14(04.38%)	2(01.67%)	4(02.22%)	—	20(03.23%)
18000 - 20000	6(01.88%)	—	—	—	6(00.97%)
20000 & above	—	—	—	—	-

General Group (N=320)

Type of Family

It could be seen from the Table 12.6 that 193(60.31%) drug users general group of students reported to be belonging to nuclear family structure and 127(39.69%) users group of students belonged to joint family structure.

Father's Occupation

40.94% of users group students had their parents working in government service, 25.94% of users' general group students had their parents' occupation in private service either working independently or in private sector organizations and 33.13% of students reported to be belonging from business class family.

Family Income

It could be seen from the Table 12.6 that 8.13% of students had their family income ranging from Rs 0-2000, 8.44% of students had their family income ranging Rs. 2000-4000, 14.06% students' family income ranged Rs. 4000 to Rs. 6000, 26.88% of students of users general group had their family income ranging from Rs. 6000 to Rs. 8000, 23.13% students' family income ranged Rs 8000-10000, 6.56% of students reported to have family income ranging Rs 10,000 to 12,000. 5.31% of students had their family income of Rs. 14000 to 16000 whereas 4.38% of students reported to have

TABLE 12.7

Percentage of Cases in Respect of Various Background Variables of Non-User Group

Variables	*General N=450*	*Medical N=205*	*Engineering N=195*	*Nursing N=130*	*Total N=980*
Types of Family					
Nuclear	329(73.11%)	157(76.59%)	152(77.95%)	63(48.46%)	701(71.53%)
Joint	121(26.89%)	48(23.41%)	43(22.05%)	67(51.54%)	279(28.46%)
Father's Occupation					
Govt. Service	175(38.89%)	84(40.98%)	70(35.89%)	58(44.62%)	387(39.49%)
Pvt. Service	142(31.56%)	82(40.00%)	68(34.87%)	55(42.31%)	347(35.41%)
Business	133(29.56%)	39(19.02%)	57(29.23%)	17(13.08%)	246(25.10%)
Family Income					
0 - 2000	67(14.89%)	32(15.61%)	19(09.74%)	34(29.23%)	156(15.92%)
2000 - 4000	79(17.56%)	31(15.12%)	25(12.82%)	55(42.31%)	190(19.39%)
4000 - 6000	91(20.22%)	43(20.98%)	41(21.03%)	20(15.38%)	195(19.90%)
6000 - 8000	129(28.67%)	64(31.22%)	61(31.28%)	17(13.08%)	271(27.65%)
8000 - 10000	57(12.67%)	17(08.29%)	32(16.41%)	—	106(10.82%)
10000 - 12000	10(02.22%)	08(03.90%)	08(04.10%)	—	26(02.65%)
12000 - 14000	2(00.44%)	—	2(01.03%)	—	04(00.41%)
14000 - 16000	6(01.33%)	5(02.44%)	6(03.08%)	—	17(01.73%)
16000 - 18000	7(01.56%)	—	1(00.51%)	—	8(00.82%)
18000 - 20000	2(00.44%)	—	—	—	2(00.20%)
20000 & above	—	5(02.44%)	—	—	5(00.51%)

their family income ranging Rs. 16000 - 18000. It is important to mention here that few students reported that their family income ranged Rs. 12000 - 14000, 18000 - 20000 respectively. None of the users from general group reported their family income ranged above Rs. 20000.

Medical Group (N=120)

Type of Family

It could be seen from the Table 12.6 that 68.33% of medical drug user students have been found to be belonging to nuclear type of family and 31.67% from user group of students reported to belong to joint family structure.

Father's Occupation

It could also be observed from this Table that 36.67% of user group of students had their parents in government service, 30% of this group of user students had their father's occupation in private service whereas 33.33% of students had their father's occupation purely from business.

Family Income

15% of students are found to have their family income ranging from Rs. 0 to 2000, 15.83% of students reported their family income ranged from Rs. 2000-4000 and 19.17% students had their family income which ranged from Rs. 4000-6000. A large number of students, i.e. 29.17% reported to have their family income ranged from Rs. 6000-8000, 15.83% students had their family income ranging between Rs. 8000-10000, whereas very few students have been found to have their family income, i.e., 3.33%, which ranged from Rs. 10000 to 12000 and 16000 to 18000, 1.67%.

Engineering Group (N=180)

Type of Family

From Table 12.6, it could be seen that 68.78% of students who belonged to this group were reported from nuclear family background and rest of the students of this group from joint family background as the obtained percentages are 32.22%.

Father's Occupation

38.33% of students had their father's occupation in government service, 35.56% students, and 26.11% students had their parent's occupation which were reported by them, i.e. private service, business respectively.

Family Income

It could be seen from the Table 12.6 that a large number of students of this group, i.e. 35% reported to have their family income ranging from Rs. 6000 to 8000, 23.89% of students had their family income which ranged 4000-6000, whereas very little variation was found between the income group of Rs. 0-2000 and Rs. 2000-4000 as the obtained percentages are 12.78%, 13.33% reported respectively.

It may be mentioned here that very few students were reported to have their family income between 8000-10000, 10000-12000, 12000-14000, 14000-16000, 16000-18000. The obtained percentages are 8.33%, 2.22%, 56%, 1.67%, 2.22% respectively as shown in Table 12.6.

Nursing Group (N=130)

It is essential to mention here that no use of drugs were reported by this group. This group is purely a non-abuser group and will be discussed later on.

Total sample (N=620)

It is also to be mentioned here that total sample of drug abusers group consisted of 620 students and frequency of each group of students have already been presented. The findings in relation to background variables will now be presented in Table 12.7.

Table 12.7 shows the clear picture of the non-abuser group where percentage of cases in respect of various important and relevant background variables have been presented.

General Group (N=450)

Type of Family

In this group, 73.11% of students were hailing from nuclear family and the rest of students were from joint family structure.

Father's Occupation

38.89% students had their father's occupation in government service, whereas, 31.56% of students reported to have their parent's occupation in private sectors. Rest of students were from business class family. The obtained percentage is 29.56%.

Family Income

It could be seen from this Table that maximum number of students in this general group, i.e. 28.67% had their family income

TABLE 12.8

Percentage of Cases who Admitted Drug use by Their Parents

Variables	*General N=770*	*Medical N=325*	*Engineering N=375*	*Nursing N=130*	*Total N=1600*
Drug abuse by parents and other family members					
Tobacco	179(23.25%)	104(32.00%)	70(18.67%)	16(12.31%)	69(23.06%)
Alcohol	55(07.14%)	22(06.77%)	28(07.47%)	9(06.92%)	114(07.13%)
Drug	—	—	—	—	—
Tobacco & alcohol	22(02.86%)	5(01.54%)	2(00.53%)	—	29(01.81%)
Alcohol & drugs	—	—	—	—	—
Alcohol, drugs & tobacco	—	—	—	—	—

TABLE 12.9

Drug Users and Non-Users' Physical Health

Drug User Group

Variables	*General N=320*	*Medical N=120*	*Engineering N=180*	*Nursing N=0*	*Total N=620*
Excellent	17(05.31%)	15(12.50%)	17(09.44%)	—	49(07.90%)
Good	128(40.00%)	52(43.33%)	56(31.11%)	—	236(38.07%)
Average	99(30.94%)	23(19.17%)	64(35.56%)	—	186(30.00%)
Poor	60(18.75%)	30(25.00%)	22(12.22%)	—	112(18.06%)
Very poor	16(05.00%)	—	21(11.67%)	—	37(05.97%)

Non-Users Group

Variables	*General N=450*	*Medical N=205*	*Engineering N=195*	*Nursing N=130*	*Total N=980*
Excellent	90(20.00%)	57(27.80%)	51(26.15%)	20(15.38%)	218(22.24%)
Good	202(44.89%)	118(57.56%)	107(54.87%)	45(34.62%)	472(48.16%)
Average	82(18.22%)	30(14.63%)	37(18.05%)	33(25.38%)	182(18.57%)
Poor	53(11.78%)	—	—	32(24.62%)	85(08.67%)
Very poor	23(05.11%)	—	—	—	23(02.35%)

ranging between Rs. 6000 to Rs. 8000, 20.22% of students ranged between the family income category, i.e. 4000 to 6000, 17.56% students had their family income which was ranged Rs. 2000 to Rs. 4000, whereas 14.89% students were reported to have their family income not more than Rs. 2000. It is to be mentioned here that few students of this particular group reported to have their family income between 8000-10000 (12.67%), 10000-12000 (2.22%), 12000-14000(.44%), 14000-16000(1.33%), 16000-18000 (1.56%) and 18000-20000 (.44%).

Medical Group (N=205)

Type of Family

It could be seen from the Table 12.7 that a large number of non-user medical students group were reported to be belonging to nuclear family structure. Very few students belonged to joint family structure and the percentage is 23.41%.

Father's Occupation

40.98% students had their parents working in government service and 40% students group have their parents in private service. Rest of the students of this group were from business class families, i.e. 19.02%.

Family Income

From the Table 12.7, it can be noticed that 31.22% medical students had their family income between the income group range of Rs. 6000 to Rs. 8000; 20.98% students reported to have their family income ranging between Rs. 4000-6000, whereas 15.61% and 15.12% of medical non-user group were found to have their family income in the range of Rs. 0-2000, and 2000-4000 respectively. Only few number of medical non-user students reported to have their family income in between the income group which were ranged between Rs. 8000-10000 (8.29%), 10,000-12,000 (3.90%), 14,000-16,000 (2.44%), 20,000 & above (2.44%) respectively.

Engineering Group (N=195)

Type of Family

It could be seen from the Table 12.7 that a large number of engineering non-users group were reported to be belonging from the nuclear family structure, i.e. 77.95% and rest of the students were reported to be from joint family structure (23.41%).

Father's Occupation

35.89% students are found to have their fathers in government service, 34.87% students reported their father's occupation, i.e., private service, whereas 29.23% were reported to be from business class family, as is evident from the Table 12.7.

Family Income

31.28%, 21.03%, 16.41%, 12.82% of non-user engineering group students reported to have their family income between the income category which ranged between Rs. 6000-8000, 4000-6000, 8000-10000, 2000-4000 respectively. On the other hand, few number of students had their family income which ranged between Rs. 10,000-12000(4.10%), 12000-14000(1.03%), 14000-16000(3.08%), 16000-18000(.51%) respectively.

Nursing Group (N=130)

Only the nursing group among all the students reported to be a non-user group. This sub-sample consisted of one hundred and thirty students.

Type of Family

It could be seen from the Table 12.7 that 48.46% of students are found to belong to nuclear family structure and 51.54% students reported to be from joint family structures.

Father's Occupation

44.62%, 42.31%, 13.08% students of this group reported to have their father's occupations as Govt. service, Pvt. service, Business respectively, as shown in Table 12.7.

Family Income

Table 12.7 also shows a clear picture regarding the family income of nursing group. A large number of students, i.e. 42.31% students had their family income which ranged between Rs. 2000 to Rs. 4000, whereas 29.23% students reported to have their family income which ranged not more than Rs. 2000. 15.38% and 13.08% students reported to have their family income between the income category of Rs. 4000-6000 and 6000-8000 only.

Total Sample (N=980)

Break-up of the sample (Non-user group) has already been presented. Description of total sample can also be seen from Table 12.7.

Table 12.8 indicates drug abuse by parents and other family members. Mostly students reported their father and other family members as taking tobacco and alcohol. 23.25% of general group students, 32% of medical students, 18.67% engineering students, and 12.31% nursing group students were found to have reported that tobacco was taken by their parents and other family members. Moreover, 7.14% students of general group, 6.77% medical students, 7.47% engineering students and 6.92% nursing students reported their father and other family member taking alcohol, whereas 2.86% students of general group, 1.54% of medical students reported tobacco and alcohol use by their parents and other family members. None of them reported the use of any other drug by their parents, brothers/sisters or friends.

Table 12.9 clearly reveals the fact regarding the drug users and non-users' physical health. Comparison between users and non-users of each group will be presented step by step. 5.31% students of general users' group reported to be in excellent physical health, whereas 20% of non-users group students were found to

TABLE 12.10

Drug Users and Non-Users' Mental Health

Drug User Group

Variables	*General N=320*	*Medical N=120*	*Engineering N=180*	*Nursing N=0*	*Total N=620*
Excellent	45(14.06%)	28(23.33%)	22(12.22%)	—	95(15.32%)
Good	151(47.19%)	62(51.67%)	115(63.89%)	—	328(52.90%)
Average	101(31.56%)	30(25.00%)	24(13.33%)	—	155(25.00%)
Poor	14(04.38%)	—	19(10.56%)	—	33(05.32%)
Very poor	9(02.81%)	—	—	—	9(01.45%)

Non-Users Group

Variables	*General N=450*	*Medical N=205*	*Engineering N=195*	*Nursing N=130*	*Total N=980*
Excellent	139(30.89%)	70(34.15%)	62(30.24%)	35(26.92%)	306(31.22%)
Good	149(33.11%)	100(48.78%)	97(49.47%)	30(23.08%)	376(38.37%)
Average	94(20.89%)	35(17.07%)	36(18.46%)	36(27.69%)	201(20.51%)
Poor	68(15.11%)	—	—	29(22.31%)	97(09.90%)
Very poor	—	—	—	—	—

have excellent physical health. Similarly, 40% students of users' general group and 44.89% students of non-users' group were found to have good physical health. 18.22% non-users' general group students are found to have average physical health which is comparatively low from students drug users' general group (30.94%). 18.75% students of users' general group and 11.78% non-users' general group reported to have poor physical health. It is interesting to point out that 5% students of users' general group and 5.11% students of non-users general group were found to have very poor physical health.

It could also be observed from Table 12.9 that 27.80% students of medical non-users' group in comparison to 12.5% students of drug users' medical group reported to have excellent physical health. 57.56% students of non-users' medical group in comparison to 43.33% students of medical drug users' group have been found to have good physical health, whereas 19.17% of medical drug users students in comparison to 14.63% non-users' medical group students were found to have average physical health. It is clear from the Table that users and non-users groups of students differ in terms of their physical health. It is important to point out that only 25% students of medical group drug users have reported poor physical health.

Drug users and non-users groups of engineering students also differ in terms of their physical health. Table 12.9 shows that 26.15% students of non-users' engineering group in comparison to 9.44% students of engineering drug users group reported to have excellent physical health. 54.87% students of non-users' engineering group and 31.11% students of engineering drug users group are found to have good physical health which indicated differences between users and non-users' physical health, whereas 35.56% students of engineering drug users group in comparison to 18.05% students of non-users engineering group had shown to have average physical health. Moreover, 12.22% and 11.67% students from drug users engineering group reported to have poor and very poor physical health, respectively. But none of the students from non-user engineering group had shown any sign of poor and very poor physical health, as is evident from Table 12.9.

It is important to mention here that nursing group had not reported to have taken any drug, hence, this sub-sample group of students fall under the category of non-users group. 15.38%,

34.62% and 25.38% students reported to have their physical health as excellent, good and average, respectively. However, 24.62% students were found to have poor physical health.

The overall picture of the results have clearly shown that there is a difference between drug users group and non-users group in terms of physical health. 22.24% students of non-users group are found to have excellent physical health, in comparison to drug users group where the finding is 7.90%. 48.16% students of non-users group in comparison to drug users group (38.07%) reported to have good physical health, whereas 18.57% non-users students and 30% drug users students were found to have average physical health (Table 12.9). 8.67% non-users students and 18.06% drug users students reported to have poor physical health. Moreover, 5.97% drug users students reported very poor physical health in comparison to non-users' physical health (2.35%).

Table 12.10 also displays clear information regarding the drug abusers and non-abusers' mental health.

30.89% non users' general group of students are found to have excellent mental health in comparison to drug users of general group, i.e., 14.06%. On the other hand 47.19% students of general users group reported to have good mental health, 31.56% drug users of general group students and 20.89% students of non-users group had reported their average mental health. 15.11% students from non-users general group students reported to have poor mental health, although 4.38% students from users group of general students have reported to have poor mental health. Only 2.81% students of general drugs users group reported to have very poor mental health (Table 12.10).

34.15% medical students of non users' group are found to have excellent mental health in comparison to 23.33% medical students from drug users group which is relatively low from the non-users' group of medical students; 51.67% medical students of drug users group in comparison to non-users' group of medical students (48.78%) are found to have good mental health, whereas 25% medical students of drug users group were found to have average mental health in comparison to non-users' group of medical students (17.07%) which are relatively low from drug users group.

30.24% engineering students from non-users' group were found to have excellent mental health in comparison to 12.22%

engineering students from drug users group. It is interesting to note that 63.89% engineering students of drug users group are found to have good mental health which is comparatively high from the engineering students of non-users' group, i.e. 49.74%, whereas 18.46% engineering students from non-users' group were reported to have average mental health in comparison to engineering students of drug users group, i.e. 13.33%. Only 10.56% engineering students from drug users group admitted to have poor mental health. As far as non-users' group of engineering students are concerned, it was found that none of them were found to have poor mental health (Table 12.10).

It may be mentioned here again that nursing group of students did not report to have taken any type of drug. Therefore, this group will fall under the category of non-users' group, of which 26.92% nursing students reported to have excellent mental health; 23.08% were also found to have good mental health, whereas 27.69% nursing students appeared to have average mental health. Only 22.31% nursing students were found to have poor mental health. Table 12.10 also reveals the overall picture of drug users' and non-users' mental health.

Results at a Glance

By and large the summary of the results can be presented as follows :

(i) Total students surveyed = 1600

(ii) Total number of drug abusers = 620

(iii) Total number of students using hard drugs = 307 (19.19%)

(iv) Total number of students using soft drugs (tobacco chewing/ smoking) =313(19.56%).

(v) Total number of students using more than one drug (soft drug followed by hard drug) = 34 (2.13%).

(vi) Most commonly used hard drugs by the students : Alcohol (11.69%), tranquillizers (2.38%), amphetamines (0.88%), opiates (0.69%), cannabis (0.69%), barbiturates (0.38%) and sedatives (0.38%).

PREVALENCE RATE OF DRUG-ABUSE AMONG "TOTAL SAMPLE" OF STUDENTS. (N=1600)

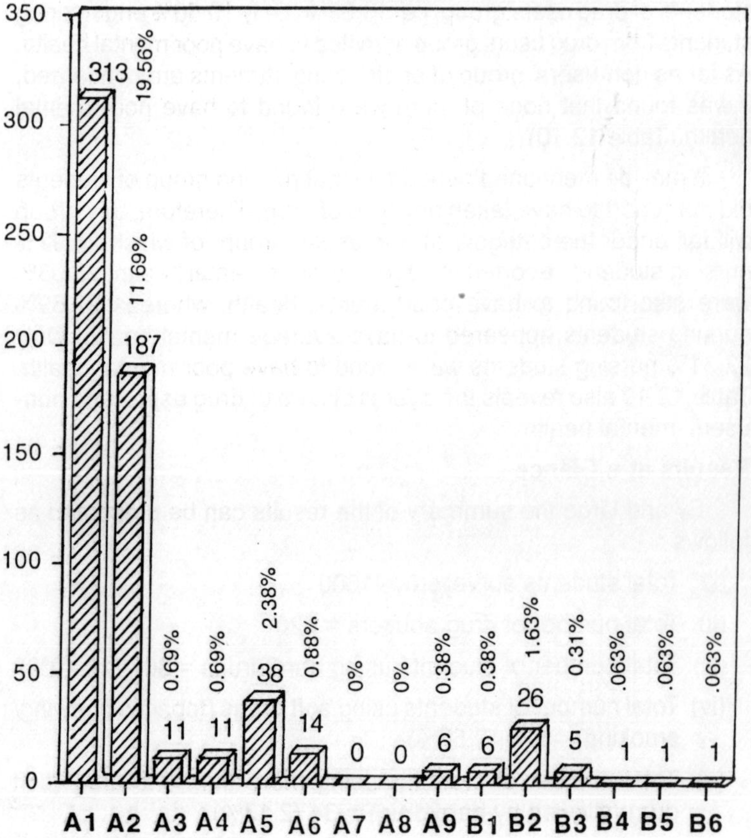

A1 = Tobacco
A2 = Alcohol
A3 = Opiates
A4 = Cannabis
A5 = Tranquilizers
A6 = Amphetamines
A7 = Opium
A8 = Heroin
A9 = Barbiturate
B1 = Sedatives
B2 = Cigarette and Alcohol
B3 = Cigarette and Cannabis
B4 = Cigarette and Tranquilizers
B5 = Cigarette and Amphetamine
B6 = Cigarette, Alcohol and Cannabis

PREVALENCE RATE OF DRUG-ABUSE AMONG "GENERAL GROUP" OF STUDENTS. (N=770)

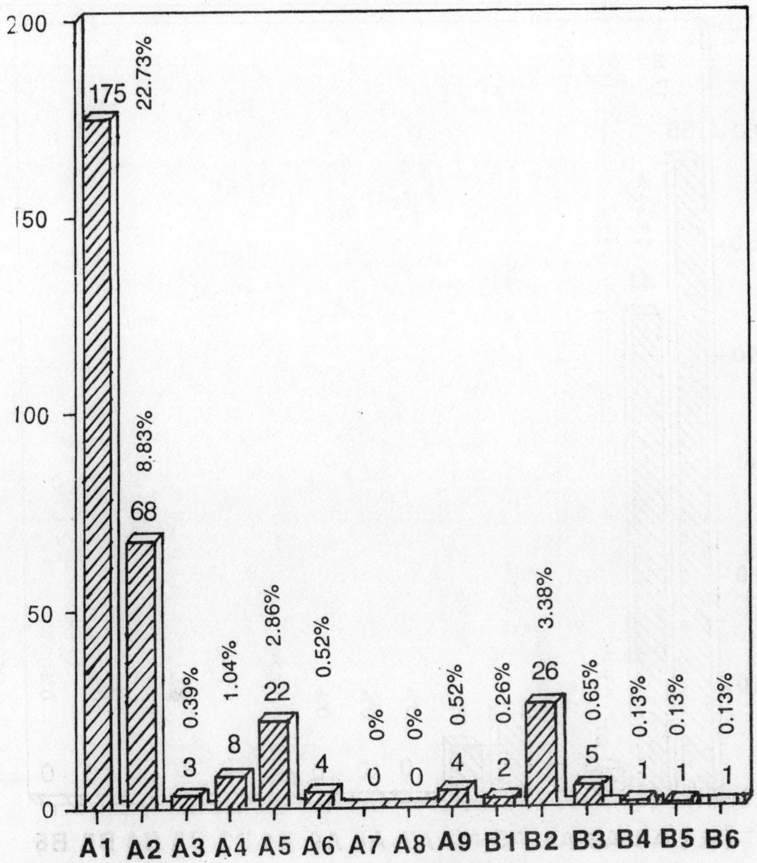

A1 = Tobacco
A2 = Alcohol
A3 = Opiates
A4 = Cannabis
A5 = Tranquilizers
A6 = Amphetamines
A7 = Opium
A8 = Heroin
A9 = Barbiturate
B1 = Sedatives
B2 = Cigarette and Alcohol
B3 = Cigarette and Cannabis
B4 = Cigarette and Tranquilizers
B5 = Cigarette and Amphetamine
B6 = Cigarette, Alcohol and Cannabis

PREVALENCE RATE OF DRUG-ABUSE AMONG "MEDICAL GROUP" OF STUDENTS. (N=325)

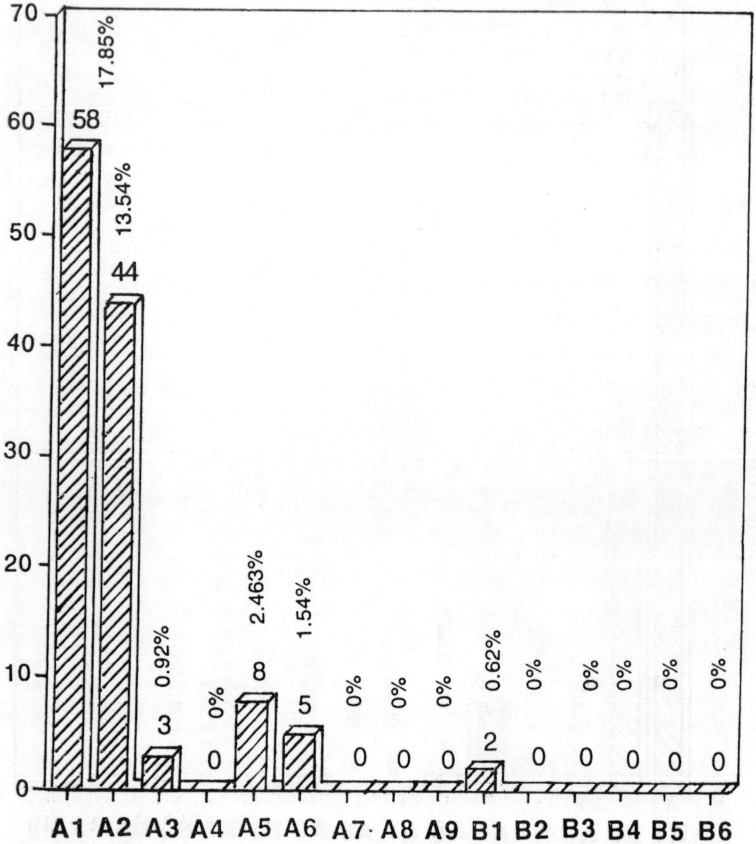

A1 = Tobacco
A2 = Alcohol
A3 = Opiates
A4 = Cannabis
A5 = Tranquilizers
A6 = Amphetamines
A7 = Opium
A8 = Heroin
A9 = Barbiturate
B1 = Sedatives
B2 = Cigarette and Alcohol
B3 = Cigarette and Cannabis
B4 = Cigarette and Tranquilizers
B5 = Cigarette and Amphetamine
B6 = Cigarette, Alcohol and Cannabis

PREVALENCE RATE OF DRUG-ABUSE AMONG "ENGINEERING GROUP" OF STUDENTS. (N=375)

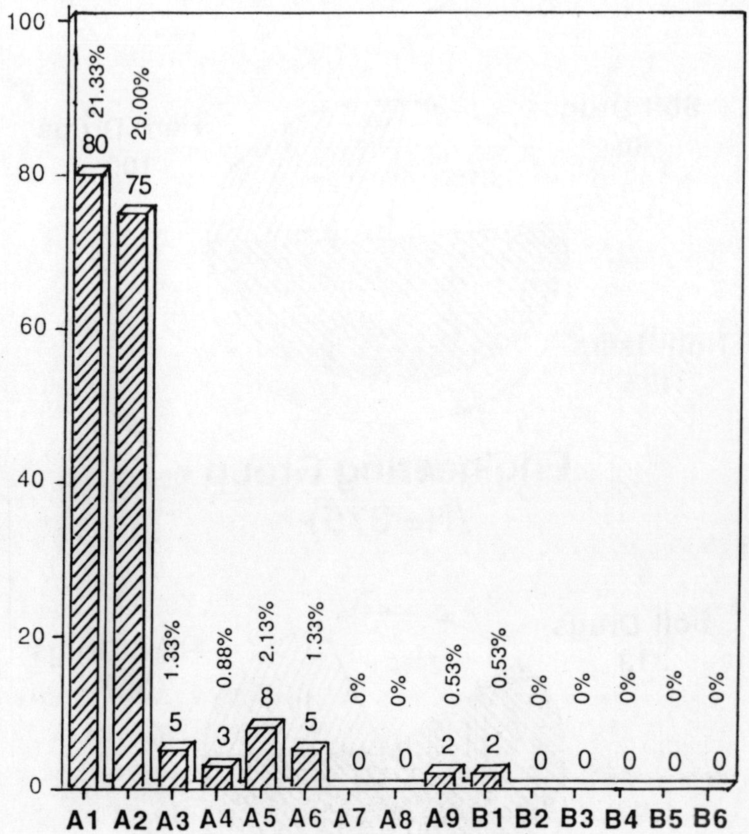

A1 = Tobacco
A2 = Alcohol
A3 = Opiates
A4 = Cannabis
A5 = Tranquilizers
A6 = Amphetamines
A7 = Opium
A8 = Heroin
A9 = Barbiturate
B1 = Sedatives
B2 = Cigarette and Alcohol
B3 = Cigarette and Cannabis
B4 = Cigarette and Tranquilizers
B5 = Cigarette and Amphetamine
B6 = Cigarette, Alcohol and Cannabis

PREVALENCE RATE OF THE USE OF HARD-DRUGS AND SOFT-DRUGS AMONG DIFFERENT GROUP OF STUDENTS

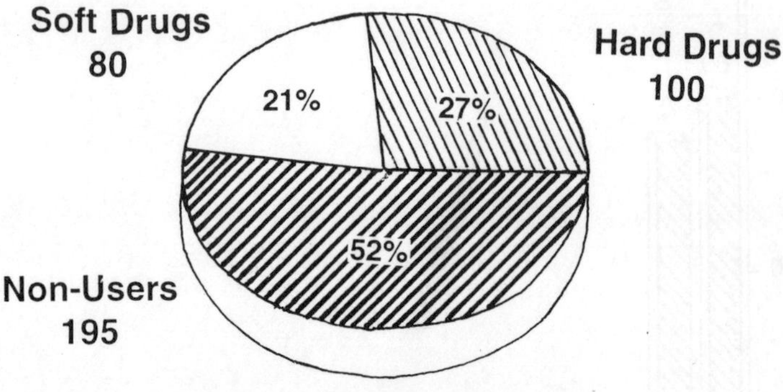

Engineering Group
(N= 375)

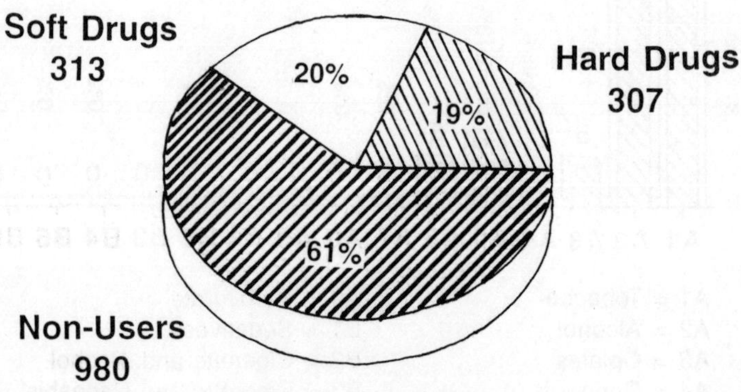

Total Group
(N= 1600)

PREVALENCE RATE OF THE USE OF HARD-DRUGS AND SOFT-DRUGS AMONG DIFFERENT GROUP OF STUDENTS

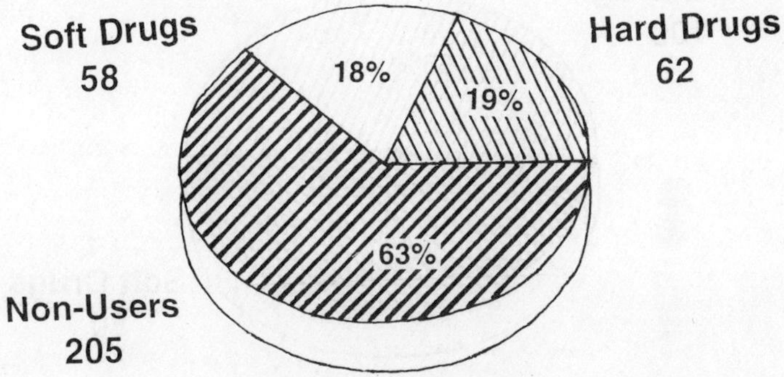

Madical Group
(N= 325)

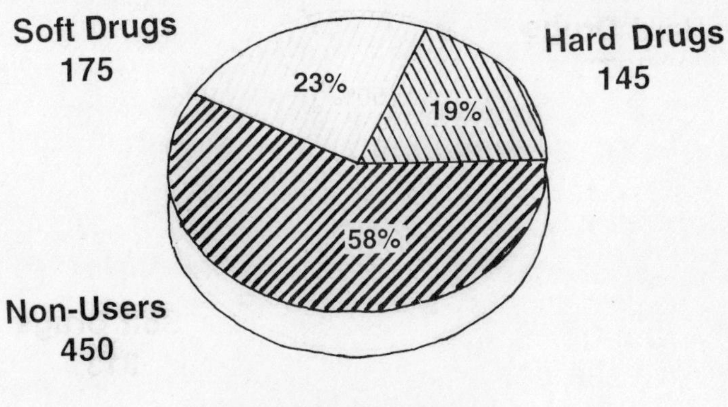

General Group
(N=770)

PERCENTAGE DISTRIBUTION OF THE USE OF HARD -DRUGS AND SOFT-DRUGS AMONG DRUG-ABUSER'S STUDENTS

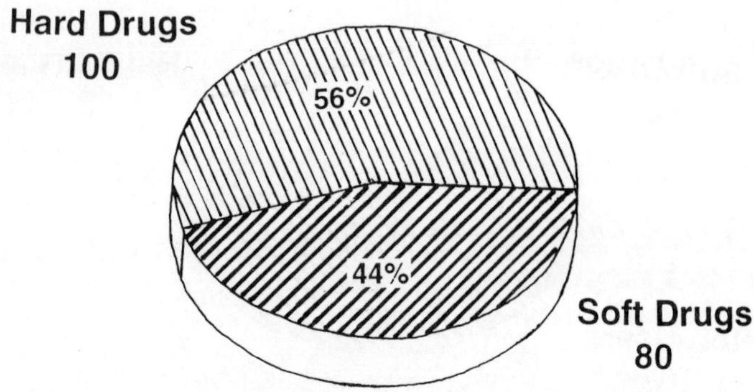

Engineering Group
(N= 180)

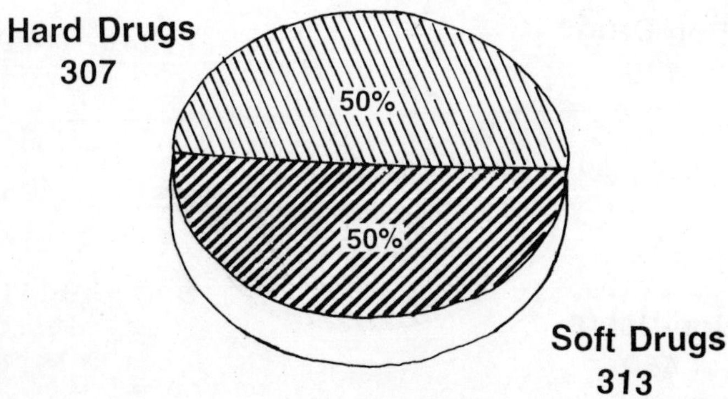

Total Group
(N= 620)

PERCENTAGE DISTRIBUTION OF THE USE OF HARD -DRUGS AND SOFT-DRUGS AMONG DRUG-ABUSER'S STUDENTS

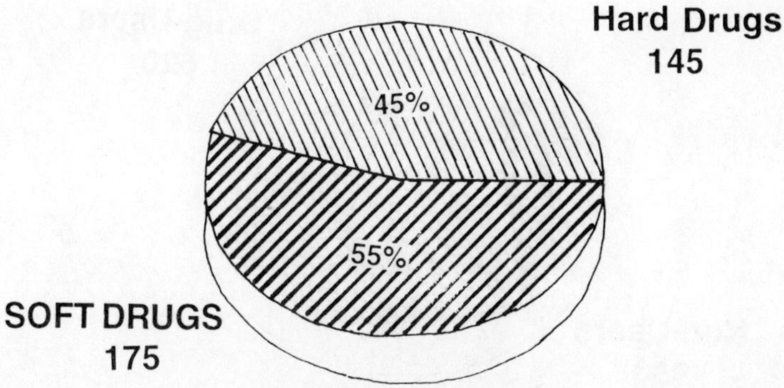

General Group
(N= 320)

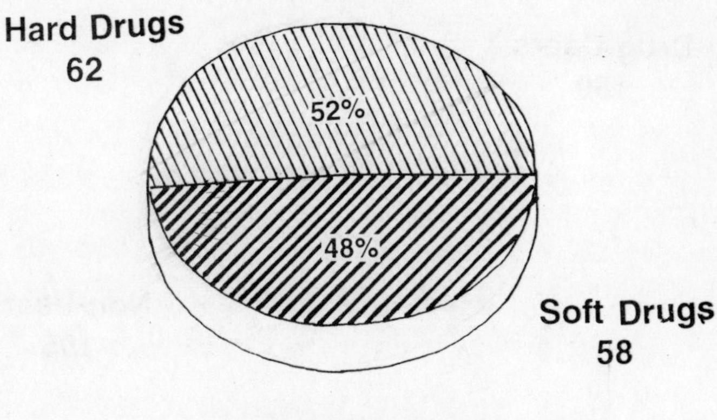

Medical Group
(N=120)

GROUP-WISE PERCENTAGE RATE OF DRUG-USERS AND NON-USERS SEPARETELY

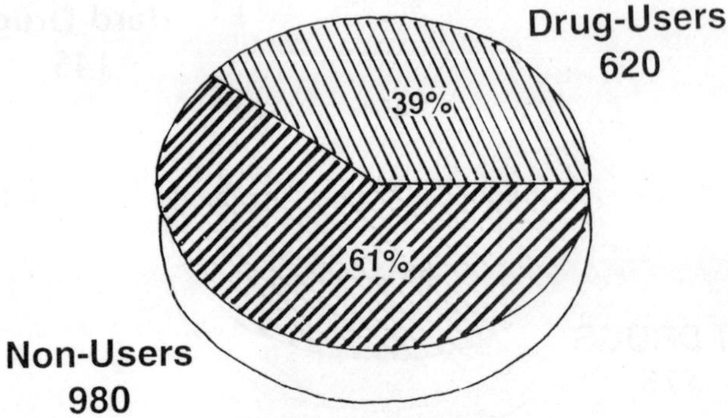

Total Group
(N= 1600)

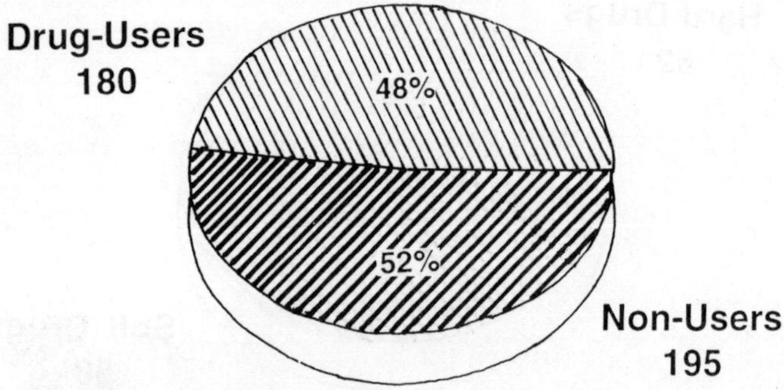

Engineering Group
(N= 375)

GROUP-WISE PERCENTAGE RATE OF DRUG-USERS AND NON-USERS SEPARETELY

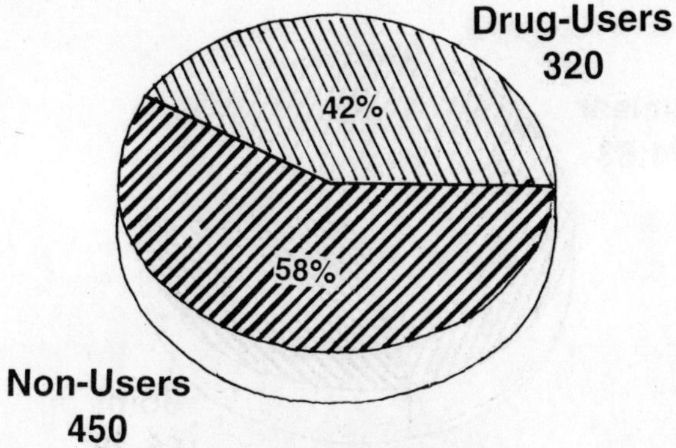

General Group
(N= 770)

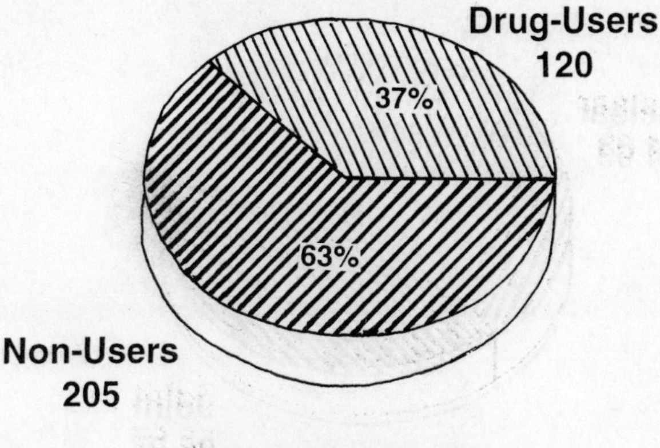

Medical Group
(N=325)

PERCENTAGE DISTRIBUTION OF TYPE OF FAMILY AMONG DRUG-USERS & NON-USERS (TOTAL SAMPLE)

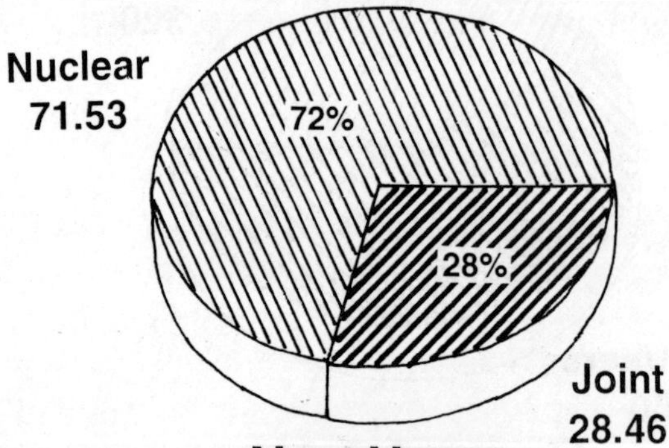

Non-Users (N= 980)

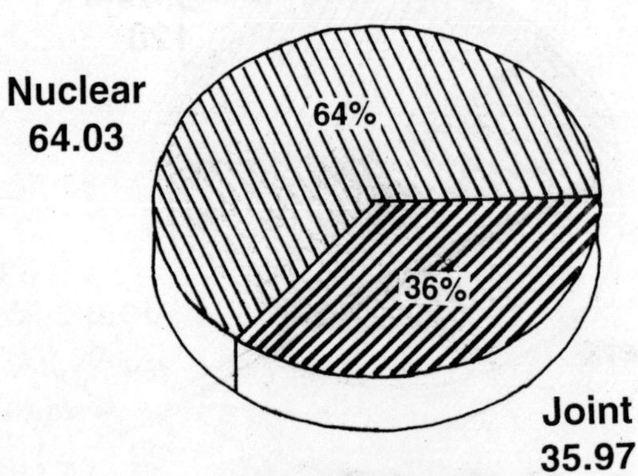

Drug-Users (N= 620)

PERCENTAGE DISTRIBUTION OF TYPE OF FAMILY AMONG DRUG-USERS & NON-USERS (GENERAL GROUP OF STUDENTS)

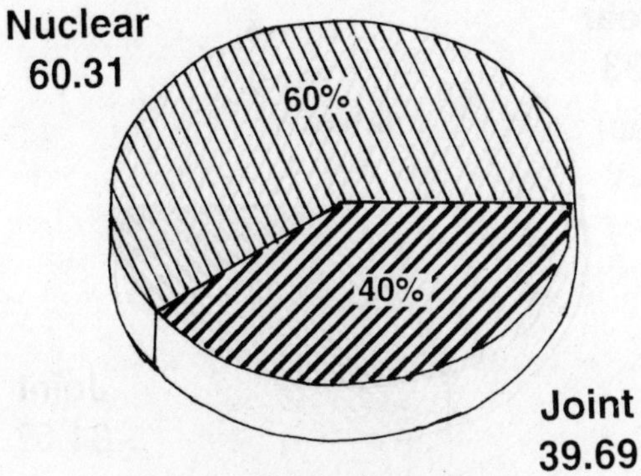

Drug-Users
(N= 320)

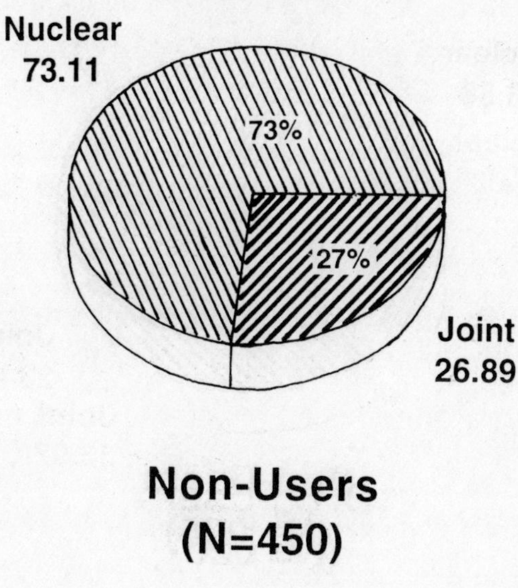

Non-Users
(N=450)

PERCENTAGE DISTRIBUTION OF TYPE OF FAMILY AMONG DRUG-USERS & NON -USERS (MEDICAL GROUP OF STUDENTS)

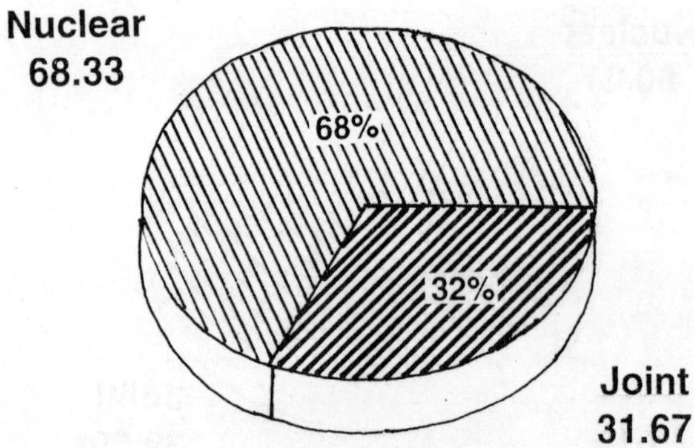

Drug-Users
(N=120)

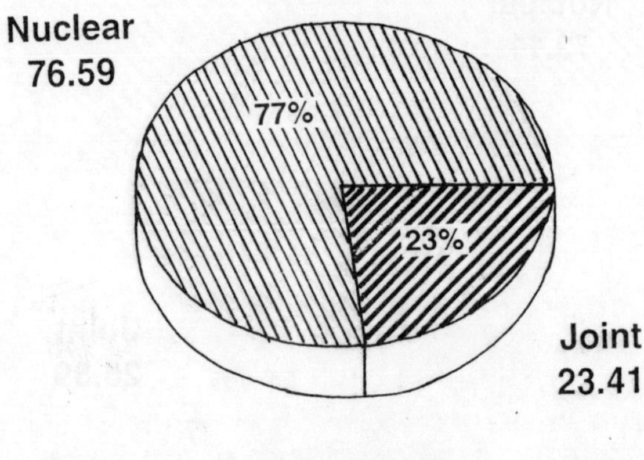

Non-Users
(N= 205)

PERCENTAGE DISTRIBUTION OF TYPE OF FAMILY OF NON-USERS GROUP (NURSING GROUP)

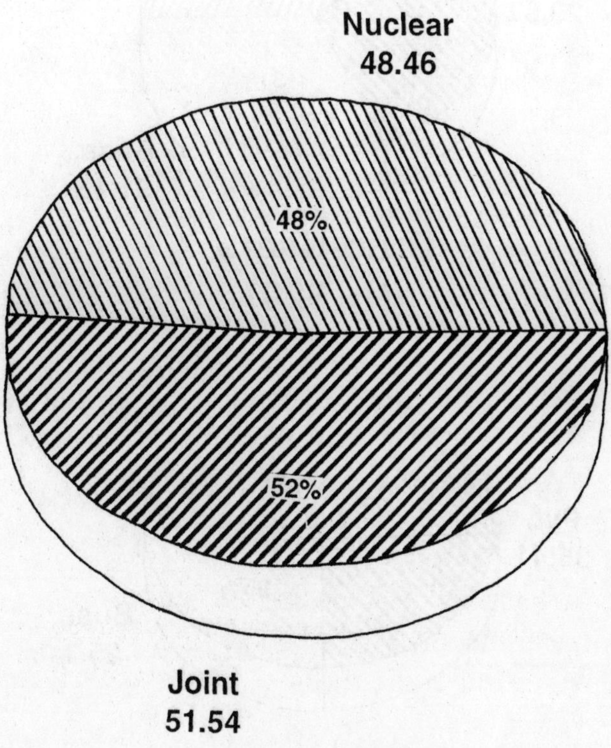

Non-Users (N= 130)

PERCENTAGE DISTRIBUTION OF FATHER'S OCCUPATION AMONG DRUG-USERS & NON-USERS (TOTAL SAMPLE)

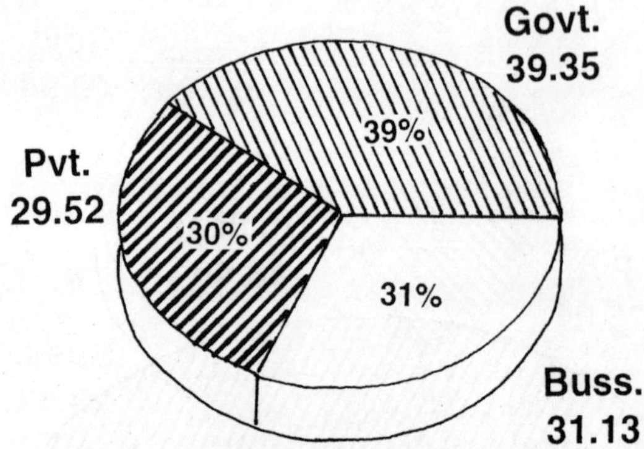

Drug-Users
(N= 620)

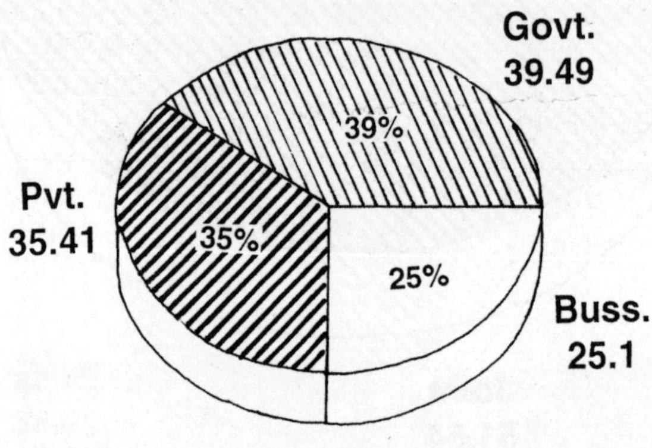

Non-Users
(N= 980)

PERCENTAGE DISTRIBUTION OF FATHER'S OCCUPATION AMONG DRUG-USERS & NON -USERS (GENERAL GROUP OF STUDENTS)

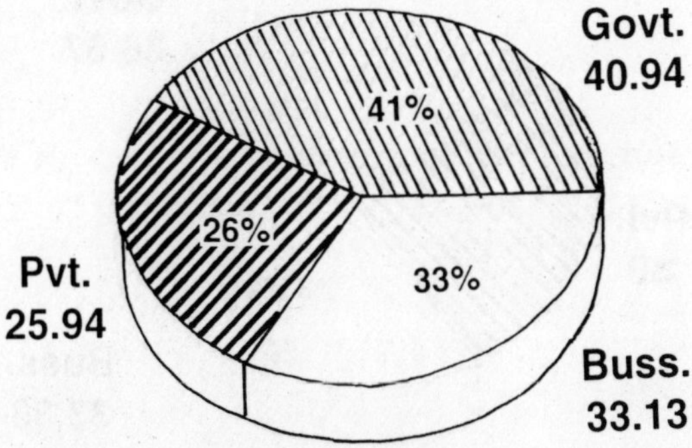

Drug-Users
(N= 320)

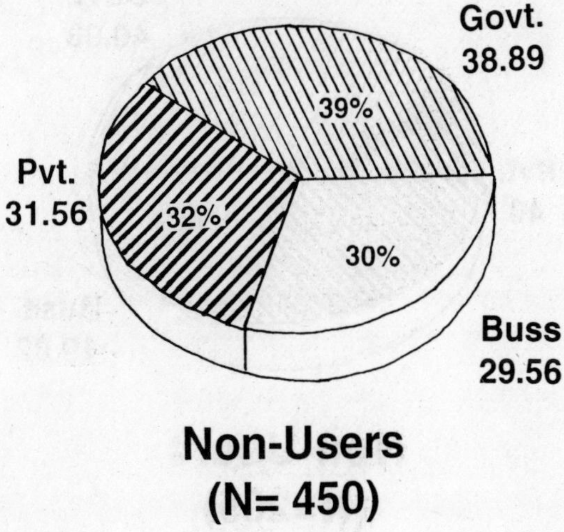

Non-Users
(N= 450)

PERCENTAGE DISTRIBUTION OF FATHER'S OCCUPATION AMONG DRUG-USERS & NON-USERS (MEDICAL GROUP OF STUDENTS)

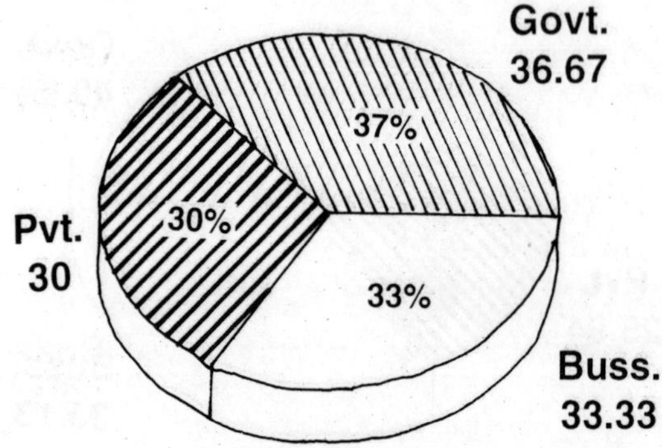

Drug-Users
(N=120)

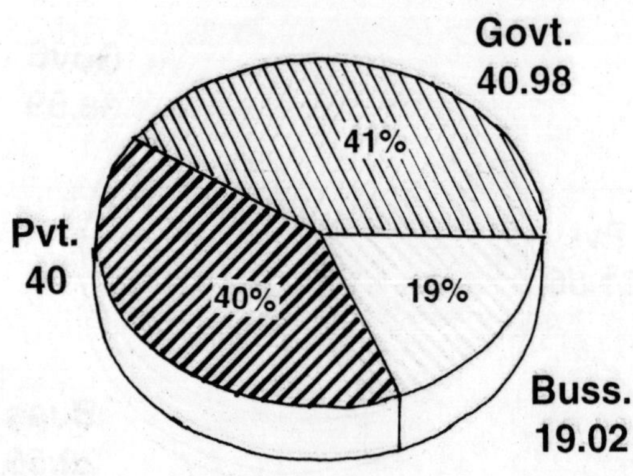

Non-Users
(N=205)

PERCENTAGE DISTRIBUTION OF FATHER'S OCCUPATION AMONG DRUG-USERS & NON-USERS (ENGINEERING GROUP OF STUDENTS)

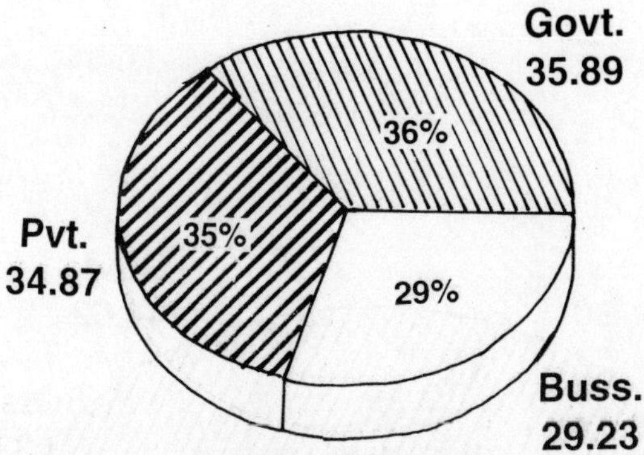

Non-Users
(N=195)

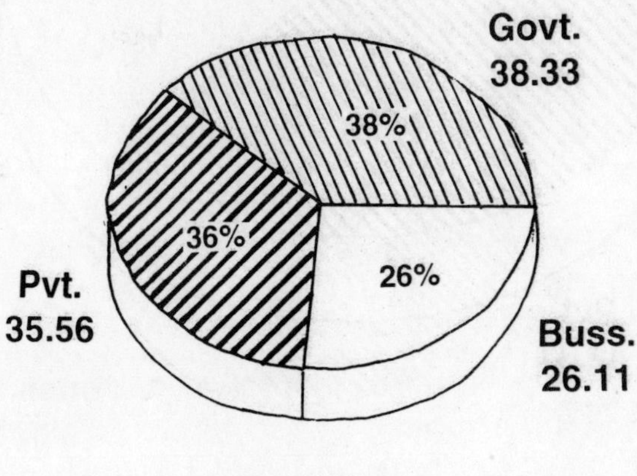

Drug-Users
(N= 180)

PERCENTAGE DISTRIBUTION OF FATHER'S OCCUPATION OF NON-USERS GROUP (NURSING GROUP OF STUDENTS)

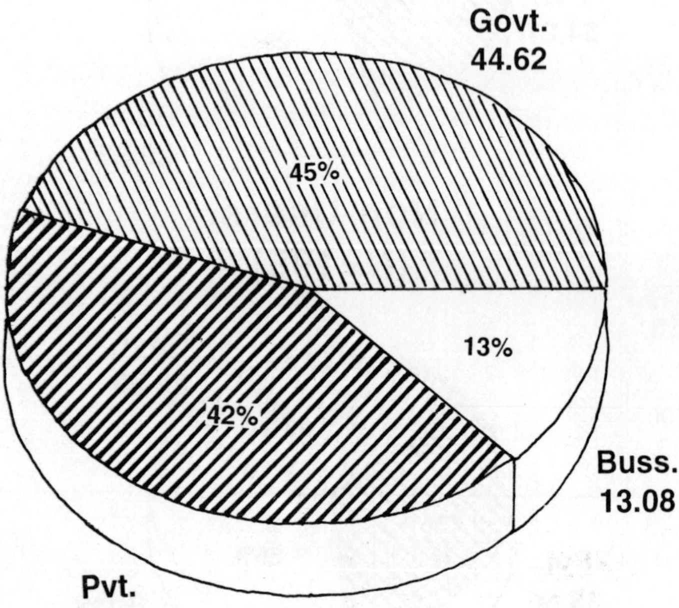

Non-Users (N=130)

FAMILY INCOME DISTRIBUTION AMONG DRUG-USERS & NON-USERS (TOTAL SAMPLE)

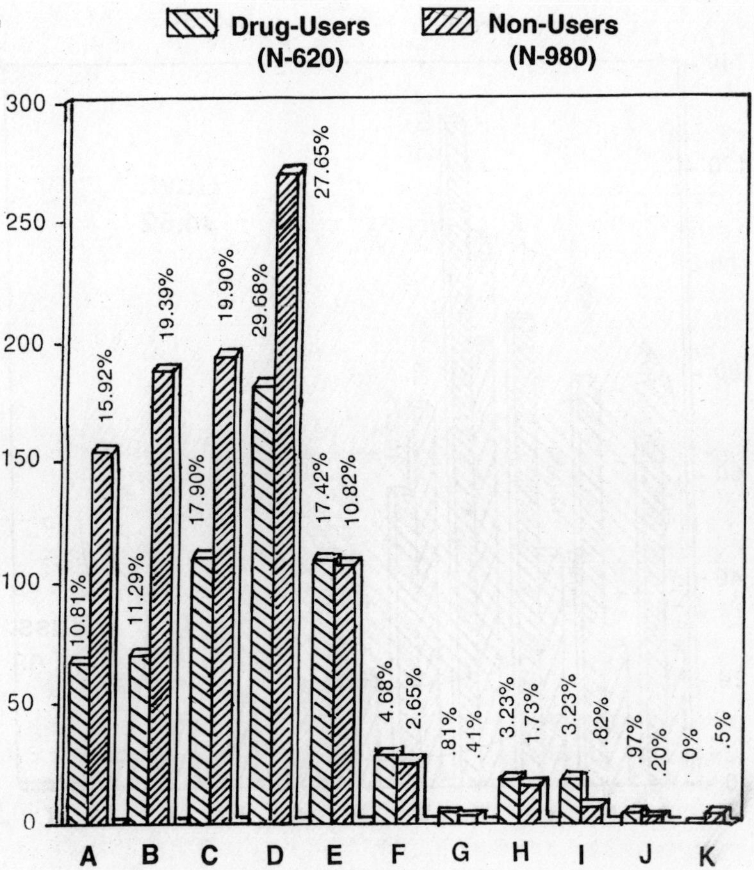

A = 0-2000 B = 2000-4000 C = 4000-6000
D = 6000-8000 E = 8000-10000 F = 10000-12000
G = 12000-14000 H = 14000-16000 I = 16000-18000
J = 18000-20000 K = 20000 & above (In Rupees)

FAMILY INCOME DISTRIBUTION AMONG DRUG-USERS & NON-USERS (GENERAL GROUP)

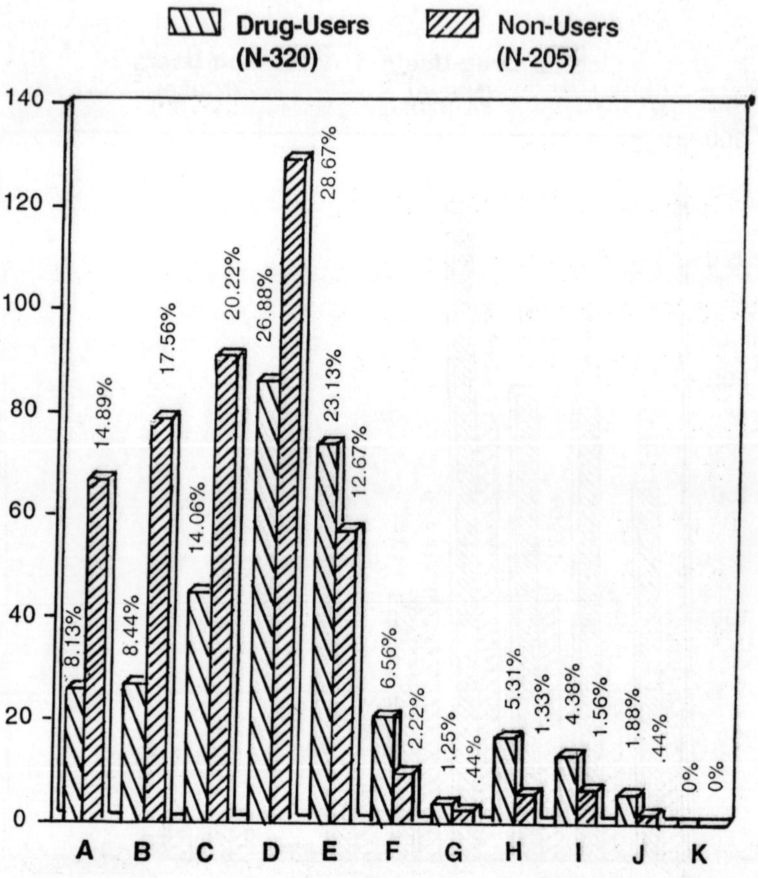

A = 0-2000 B = 2000-4000 C = 4000-6000
D = 6000-8000 E = 8000-10000 F = 10000-12000
G = 12000-14000 H = 14000-16000 I = 16000-18000
J = 18000-20000 K = 20000 & above (In Rupees)

FAMILY INCOME DISTRIBUTION AMONG DRUG-USERS & NON-USERS (MEDICAL GROUP)

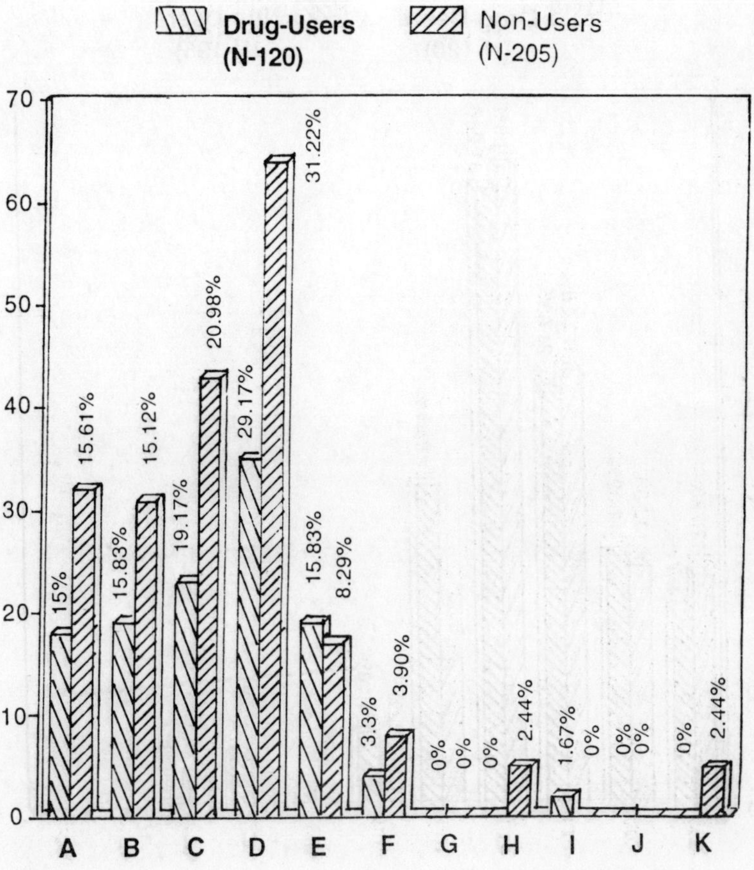

A = 0-2000 B = 2000-4000 C = 4000-6000
D = 6000-8000 E = 8000-10000 F = 10000-12000
G = 12000-14000 H = 14000-16000 I = 16000-18000
J = 18000-20000 K = 20000 & above (In Rupees)

FAMILY INCOME DISTRIBUTION AMONG DRUG-USERS & NON-USERS (ENGINEERING GP.)

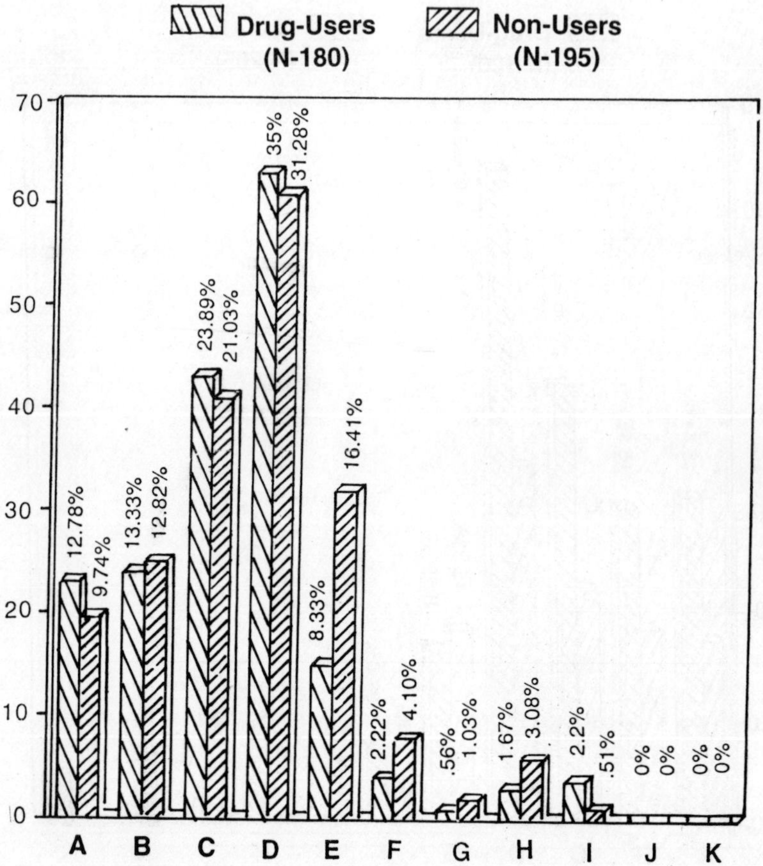

A = 0-2000 B = 2000-4000 C = 4000-6000
D = 6000-8000 E = 8000-10000 F = 10000-12000
G = 12000-14000 H = 14000-16000 I = 16000-18000
J = 18000-20000 K = 20000 & above (In Rupees)

FAMILY INCOME DISTRIBUTION OF NON-USERS GROUP (NURSING GROUP)

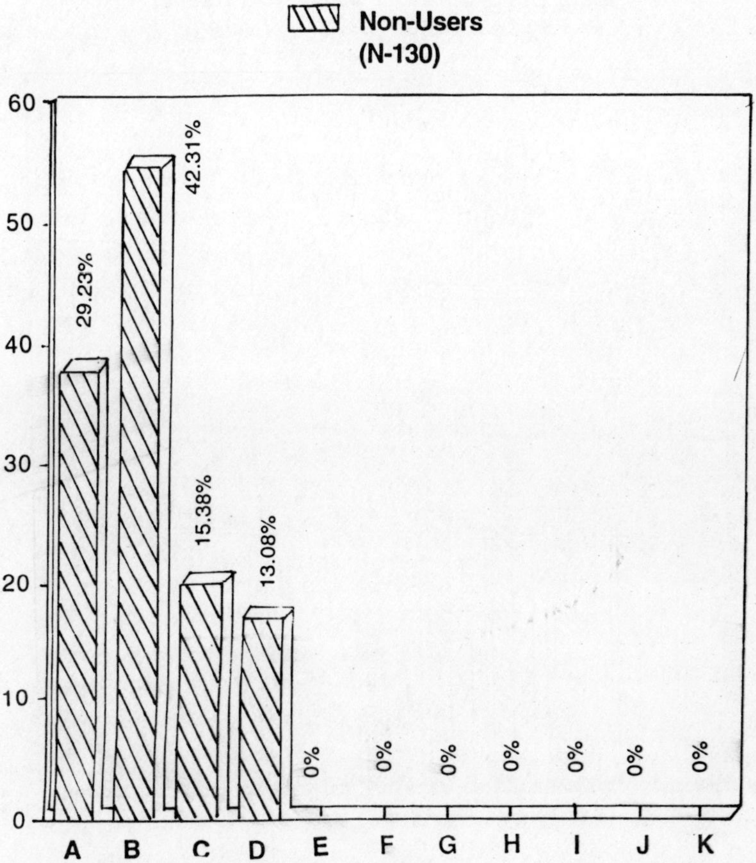

A = 0-2000 B = 2000-4000 C = 4000-6000
D = 6000-8000 E = 8000-10000 F = 10000-12000
G = 12000-14000 H = 14000-16000 I = 16000-18000
J = 18000-20000 K = 20000 & above (In Rupees)

13

DISCUSSION

It is apparent from chapters 1 to 3 that a great range of psycho-social variables can be invoked to account for variance in drug abuse. Drug-abuse behaviour is an intricately complex phenomenon and is a multidisciplinary problem.

In the present work an attempt has been made to study some of the psycho-social concomitants related to prevalence of drug abuse among the students, with the hypothesis that drug abusers of each group differ in terms of types and their uses. It is important to mention here that the present study was aimed at studying the prevalence rate of drug abuse among the different professionals and non-professional groups of Delhi University students like "general group" that included graduate and undergraduate students from arts, social sciences, natural science and also research scholars. From professional groups like medical, engineering and nursing students were taken for the study. Each group of abusers and non-abusers were identified by collecting the data through questionnaire technique. In all 1600 students were included in this study.

Tables 12.1 and 12.3 have already indicated the description of results where 320 (41.56%) students from general group (N=770) were found to have taken different types of drugs, 120 (36.92%) students from medical group reported to have taken drugs, whereas from engineering group, 180 (48%) students admitted to having taken drugs. There was only one group, i.e., nursing group, who has reported not to have taken any type of drug. It could also be seen from the Tables 12.1 and 12.3 that out of total sample (N=1600), only 620 (38.75%) students were admitted to be drug addicts. Rest of them were considered as non-abusers group. The description of the results have already been presented in Table12.5.

As far as hard and soft drugs are concerned, it is imperative to mention here that among the drug abusers, 307 (49.52%) students were found to have taken hard drugs like alcohol, opiates, cannabis, tranquillizers, amphetamines, barbiturates and sedatives. On the other hand, 313 (50.48%) students were reported to have taken soft drugs like *bidi*, cigarette, *hukka* and other tobacco substances. The description of drug-abusers in terms of their hard and soft drugs have already been highlighted in the Table 12.4 of the results section.

Whereas the Table 12.2 has already been described regarding the prevalence rate of the use of hard and soft drugs among the different groups of students as well as in the total sample, it is apparently clear from the table that the percentage rate of using soft and hard drugs is almost similar among all the groups of students with the variation of negligible percentage that may evoke any significance of difference statistically. It is important to point out that this variation seems to be a horrible sign for the society because it may lead to various psycho-social problems.

Tables 12.1 and 12.3 have clearly shown the percentage rate of drug abuse by students which differ from group to group as far as hard and soft drugs are concerned. It was observed during the investigation that generally students during the period of their university examinations, or competitive examinations are found to become more stressful than on normal days.

In the present study, four groups of students were taken in which high percentage, i.e., 48% students were recorded as drug users from engineering group, 36.92% from medical group, and 41.56% from the general group. Thus the engineering group of students are more prone to drug abuse than other groups of students. The results seem to be logical that generally engineering courses are considered as technical profession in their nature. They were found to be highly prone to addiction. Medical students are also considered as technical or professional students but it seems that their work is generally considered to be non-technical because most of the time they diagnose the patient and write case-study and report. Although, it is more important to mention here that in comparison to engineering and general groups of students, medical students are more aware about the consequences of drug usage. The general group of students were found to be more anxious as far as their careers are concerned and were reported to be drug addicts (41.56%). It is significant to note that some of the students from each group reported that hard drug intoxication gives them relaxation of the mind, free from tension and frustration. They fall asleep quickly. It is generally observed that for relaxation, relieving tension and to enjoy themselves seem to be the common feeling for starting drug abuse in a majority of students. Drugs give them relief from psychological stresses as reported by a large number of students. It is a fact that stress occurs when biological and physiological needs as well as external demands are greater than the ability of the individual to adapt. *Seley (1956)* in his pioneering work used the concept of stress in a manner relevant in social sciences. He expounded his biological concept of stress as the General Adaption Syndrome (GAS)— a three-phase response to stress that begins with an alarm, continues with resistance, and may terminate with exhaustion. According to *Panchanathan and Shanmugaganesan (1992),* stress is a reaction to something that is specific to an individual.

Tables 12.6 and 12.7 have revealed a picture regarding the various background information of all the abusers and non-abusers groups like 'general group', 'medical group', 'engineering group', and 'nursing group' of students. It is pertinent to mention that both the groups of abusers and non-abusers had shown very little difference in terms of their types of family, occupation of their father, and their family income. It is to be pointed out that in the group of drug-users only nursing group had not reported to have taken any drug. Therefore their background variables had not been mentioned (Table 12.6). The results also indicate that all the groups of students among the abusers and non-abusers belong to good family background. The group of students are economically balanced as their fathers are working either in government service or in private service. All the organizations, today, either government or private, provide handsome salary to their staff to fulfil their needs. But every moment change is brought to create congenial environment within the organization and outside the organization too. So, it is generally seen that stress occurs when any change is introduced and people become fatigued. Hence, to reduce the psychological fatigue, drugs are mainly used. In addition to this context, it is to be pointed out that to fulfil the higher demands of the society, to maintain dignity in society, to increase the family income for catering to their needs as well, generally parents and other family members are found to be more anxious and frustrated. So, they are also found to be drug users. It could be observed from the Table 12.8, that a number of parents and their family members are found to be prone to drugs. 23.6% parents and other family members consumed tobacco, 7.13% students reported the use of alcohol by their fathers, whereas 1.81% were reported having tobacco followed by alcohol. The description of the results of all the groups have been mentioned in Table 12.8. It could be observed from the results that most of the parents were having good educational background and it seems that they are aware about the consequences of drug abuse. It is also observed that all the parents were economically sound and engaged to perform their activity towards their job in planned direction. A large number of students reported about the feelings of their parents towards drugs and pointed out that drug usage is harmful for health and its usage breaks the nation's back and is wastage of money and also destroys life which leads to nation's downfall. But in spite of this a number of students from all the groups (except nursing group) were found to be drug addicts (Table 12.1). The students from business class reported to have taken drugs occasionally especially in marriage parties and religious ceremonies.

On the basis of the observations and past researches, it is witnessed that the sources of procurements of drugs are generally the friends, though, reasons like curiosity and to remove anxiety or stress are also some of the concomitants. Group membership of the intoxicant is also the other reason for taking opiates. It is mostly tried with cigarette while other pharmaceutical drugs have been taken orally in pill form. It is also observed that most of the students are in the habit of taking numerous drugs for a change. It is important to point out that in a large number of students from all the groups except nursing group reported as drug abusers, tobacco has the highest prevalence rate (19.56%), and the second is alcohol (11.69%) (Table 12.1). These drugs are easily available in market legally. It may be said that government is getting enormous profit from sale of tobacco and alcohol, and as such licences are being provided to sell these products. Even in the traditional and still conservative Indian society, where religion has been a binding force among the people, religious community has not been able to exercise its control on the mechanisms, to stop the spread of drug abuse. It was particularly true about the younger generation and the youth of every religious community seems to be equally exposed to the risk of drug abuse.

Tables 12.6 and 12.7 have also indicated the nature of family to which they belong. It is relevant to point out that like other nations of the world, India too is undergoing a major change in the nature and structure of its social institutions, particularly the family. These changes are likely to lead to far reaching consequences on the individual's aspirations and behaviour and the interaction with his environment. The joint families are breaking up under the economic and social pressures which are making rapid headway. It could be pointed out from the Tables, that most of the students surveyed (64.03%) drug addicts belonged to nuclear family structure. The results seem to be an indication that a higher proportion of addicts belonging to nuclear families may be due to lack of nurturing, insecurity, control and correction given by its members. Most of the students from non-user groups also belong to nuclear family structure but as far as drug users and non-users' family structures are concerned there is some discernible difference as is shown in Tables 12.6 and 12.7.

It is very significant to mention here that drug related problems crop up in many areas of life. The physical and mental health, work life, marital and familial relations, etc., seem to be greatly affected by drug abuse. It penetrates every area of life such as educational institutions, industry, transportation, courts, homes and cuts across social, cultural and economic lines. As far as the present study is concerned, only physical and mental health informations were asked from the students on five point scale like excellent, good, average, poor and very poor. After getting informations from the users and non-users group, a significant difference between the groups was found as is evident from (Tables 12.9 and 12.10).

Table 12.9 shows that 22.24% students from non-users groups were reported to have 'excellent' physical health, while 7.90% of drug users reported the same. Again, 48.16% students of non-users group reported to have 'good' physical health while 38.07% of drug users group reported the same. It is interesting to note that 30% students of drug users group are found to have 'average' physical health in comparison to non-users' group which is 18.57%. 18.06% students of drug users group reported to have 'poor' physical health. 5.97% students from drug users group were found to have 'very poor' physical health in comparison to non-users group (2.35%). The findings and record of each of the groups like 'general', 'medical', 'engineering' and 'nursing' have already been depicted in Table 12.9. The results revealed the fact that the students who are taking drugs (either soft drugs or hard drugs) feel guilty in general, and become anxious in particular. They are found not to have good physical health as well in comparison to non-users group.

As far as drug users' and non-users' mental health are concerned, the results of the Table 12.10 have clearly shown the fact that 31.22% students of non-users' group are found to have 'excellent' mental health in comparison to drug users group (15.32%) which is relatively low. On the other hand 52.90% of drug users group are found to have 'good' mental health which is relatively high in comparison to non-users' mental health. Again 25% students of drug users' group are also found to have 'average' mental health in comparison to drug users group (20.51%), whereas 9.90% students from non-users group reported to have 'poor' mental health in comparison to drug users (5.32%). Moreover, only 1.45% students from drug users group were reported to have 'very poor' health. The results fluctuated. The levels of mental health varied from group to group according to the nature of sample. Another finding is that the drug users' group were found to be less intelligent, emotionally immature, apprehensive, frustrated, anxious and less independent; whereas non-users' group were found to be intelligent, emotionally mature, calm and lively. They are expedient, self-assured, confident, relaxed and not frustrated. They are also found to be less anxious and independent.

Before concluding, it is necessary to throw some light on some of the observations made by the present investigator. The problem of drug abuse has been a matter of serious public concern especially in the wake of its proliferation among the youth in various sociocultural and economic strata. It is widely observed that the problem is no longer confined to a particular section or stratum of society. It, however, appears more to be concentrated in metropolitan cities, international borders and places of tourist interest.

As far as the present investigation is concerned, it can be pointed out that to secure information on the use of drugs from students is an extremely difficult task. The main problem is of identification of students who take drugs since the respondents in this study cannot be regarded as constituting a representative sample of the drug taking student population, so the findings presented in this report cannot be regarded as conclusive. However, the study does give reasonably reliable information covering psycho-socio-economic background and facts pertaining to drug use in respect of students who served as respondents in this study.

14

PSYCHOLOGICAL CHARACTERISTICS OF THE DRUG ABUSERS

The widespread abuse of drugs poses a threat to the whole world. Although in India many drugs have been used during social occasions, since time immemorial, the present-day drug abuse is a new pattern of social threat to the country. In the existing complex social conditions, the youngsters do not want to face the realities of their lives. They try to take refuge from their frustrations in drugs which stimulate and control some of their disappointments, eventually forcing them to adopt an artificial life dependent on drugs. Dissatisfaction with current life situations, the generation gap, bereavement, loneliness or just plain curiosity are some of the common reasons for drug dependence. Drug addiction may be defined as a state of periodic or persistent intoxication, detrimental to the individual, to society, or both; and is characterized by the features of (a) a strong drive, need or compulsion to continue taking the drug, (b) the development of tolerance with a tendency to increase the dose to produce desired effects, and (c) physiological and emotional dependence *(Rees, 1980).*

Individuals may become dependent on a wide variety of chemical substances, ranging from stimulants to depressants. All such drugs have at least one effect in common, in that, they are capable of creating a state of mind in certain individuals which is termed psychic dependence. This is a psychic drive which requires periodic or chronic administration of the drug either for pleasure or to avoid discomfort. Most people feel that if they take drugs only once, it will not harm them, and also, that they cannot become addicted to it. But this is not true.. Drugs are more potent now a-days than they were earlier. If one looks back 15 or 20 years ago, and compares it to the present, it is found that marijuana is ten times stronger now than it was then. Cocaine which was only 20 per cent pure 15 years ago, is now as pure as 80 per cent. It can even be found one hundred per cent pure. When people used to take heroin by injecting into a vein earlier, it was measured by 6 per cent purity, but today it is generally found at 14 per cent purity, and it is even possible to have 90 per cent purity. If the potency is that high, just taking the drug only once can kill the person *(Vohra, 1990)*. Individuals enter into the narcotic world initially by oral intake of tablets or by sniffing or inhaling. The next step usually is the skin popping or intramuscular injection of drugs, and finally for greater satisfaction, injecting it into the vein.

Broad Categories of Drugs

(a) Narcotics

The prototype drug for this group is morphine, the major active ingredient is opium (the origin of the name opiate for this family of drugs). Opium is the resinous exudate of the white poppy. Opium contains morphine as well as other psychoactive substances which can be extracted in pure form, including codeine, a widely used drug for pain and cough. Morphine can be converted into heroin (diacetylmorphine or diamorphine) by a relatively simple chemical process. In addition there are many entirely synthetic opiates, such as methadone, pethidine and dipipanone. All these substances share a capacity to relieve pain and produce a pleasant, detached, dreamy euphoria, leading to inducing physical dependence withdrawal symptoms when the drug is stopped.

(b) Depressants

This drug group includes alcohol, the barbiturates and an enormous variety of synthetic sedatives and sleeping tablets (hypnotics). These substances in common have the ability to cause a degree of drowsiness and sedation or pleasant relaxation, but may also produce disinhibition and loss of intelligence activity as a result of their depressant effect on the higher centres of the brain. They all have in common the potential to induce changes in the nervous system that lead to withdrawal syndrome, the possible seriousness of which should be emphasized, because it can be life-threatening. Minor tranquillizers of the benzodiazepine type such as diazepam or chlorodiazepoxide produce physical dependence and should be used carefully, though they are safer than barbiturates. The first barbiturate, diethylbarbituric acid (Barbitone) or Veronal, was introduced in 1903. They produce psychological as well as physical dependence. Dependence generally occurs in the emotionally maladjusted person seeking relief from unbearable feelings of tension, anxiety and inadequacy.

(c) Stimulants

(i) Cocaine : This is a psychoactive ingredient of the coca leaf. It produces a sense of exhilaration and decreased feelings of fatigue and hunger. It can cause extreme excitement and short-lasting psychotic illness. This substance has a high dependence potential although withdrawal symptoms seem to be limited to temporary feelings of fatigue, 'let-down', and depression.

(ii) Amphetamines : The amphetamines have been marketed under hundreds of different brand names and have been used as "diet pills" for the treatment of obesity. Amphetamines are currently being illegally manufactured on a large-scale in the form of amphetamine sulphate.

(iii) Caffeine : Tea and coffee contain caffeine. They are stimulants in that they alleviate mild degree of fatigue, but their mechanism of action in the body is different from cocaine and amphetamine. Generally, they produce very low levels of dependence and withdrawal symptoms, if any, seem limited to some headache and fatigue

(iv) Khat : It is widely used in countries like Ethiopia and Somalia. Khat is a shrub, the leaves of which are chewed and the juice swallowed. The active ingredients are cathine and cathinone, which produce actions similar to those of the amphetamines. Khat produces cerebral stimulation and is used to promote social interaction and release emotional tension. Among its adverse effects are insomnia, constipation and gastritis.

(d) Hallucinogens

This group includes LSD (Lysergic Acid Diethylamide), mescaline, peyote and certain other plant-derived or synthetic substances. These drugs have the capacity to induce highly complex psychological effects, including transcendental experience of "other-worldliness", hallucinations and other types of perceptual distortions. Sometimes these experiences are bizarre and frightening, and hence a 'bad trip'. Hallucinogens do not induce physical dependence.

(e) Cannabis

It is the generic name given to the drug containing plant products of Indian hemp. This plant produces an extraordinary array of psychoactive chemicals, the most important of which is tetrahydrocannabinol (THC). The dried leaves or flowering tops are often referred to as marijuana or *ganja,* although *ganja* may also have generic meaning, and the resin from the plant is referred to as *hashish* or 'hash'. *Bhang* is a drink made from cannabis. Cannabis appears to act as a depressant to some extent, but it can also have hallucinogenic effects.

(f) Volatile Inhalants

These include anaesthetic gases, glues, paint thinners and so on. They may have some depressant and anaesthetic effects, but also seem capable of producing perceptual disturbances. Their chief danger is their physical toxicity. Solvent sniffing can become a habit, and in some users a considerable degree of compulsion to continue the behaviour develops.

Routes of Administration

There are a number of ways in which a drug may be taken into the body. Drugs may be swallowed (eaten or drunk), chewed and absorbed through the lining of the nose, inhaled through the nostrils or injected beneath the skin, into the muscles, or into a vein. Some drugs can be taken in several different ways. For instance, tobacco can be chewed, sniffed as snuff or smoked or injected. These different methods of getting drugs into the body have important implications for drug-effects, risk of dependence, and risk of health. A substance that is eaten will produce effects that are less rapid on onset and less intense than, when the same drug is injected. The effect of inhalation usually falls somewhere between these two extremes, but some smoked drugs produce much the same rapid impact on the brain as intravenous injecting. As regards risks to health, the potential damage associated with the given drug is determined partly by the possible inherent toxic actions of that drug once it is circulated within the body.

Health risks are also related specifically to the route of administration. Direct effect of excessive and continued drinking can cause cancer of the gullet. Inhaled drugs and cigarette smoking carry a particular risk of damage to the lungs and bronchial cancer or chronic bronchitis. Intravenously injected drugs offer frightening risks, for instance, tetanus, viral hepatitis B, malaria and AIDS. Within a broader perspective, it is not the drug-dependence itself that is the problem, but the harm done by the continuous use of the dependence producing drug, conventionally classified as having physical, mental and social consequences. In reality, these are usually far from being compartmentalized.

Etiology of Drug Dependence

The literature on the causes of drug use and abuse is extensive. Many theories have been propounded, most of which are consistent with the characteristics and behaviour of particular sub-groups of drug-users. Different types of drug-related behaviour are reported to have different causes. Initial or experimental drug use may result from a combination of peer pressure, curiosity, price and availability. Progression to greater involvement or to dependence may be attributable to other factors, such as personality traits or social deprivation. In addition, other factors may explain why some chronic or dependent drug-users continue taking drugs in a harm-producing way while others do not. The main factors identified as contributing to drug abuse are:

1. Peer Pressure

Peer pressure has frequently been identified as a cause of initial drug use. It is widely acknowledged that the use of psychoactive drugs is commonly a facet of people's lifestyles. Those with strong affiliative needs are particularly likely to be influenced by the encouragement of their friends and associates to engage in drug-taking. Such encouragement often appears to be an important precursor of drug use. Individuals become convinced that it is attractive, safe, beneficial or prestigious before they are likely to engage in it. This process of redefinition clearly involves a departure from the 'anti-drug' views that are commonly derived from parents and other authoritative figures. Such ideas lead us to the concept of 'sub-culture', that is, a system of shared beliefs, attitudes and symbols, differentiating or partly differentiating a particular group from the larger culture.

2. Self-Medication

Many psychotropic drugs serve, only briefly, to allay anxiety and depression. Opiates give ready relief from pain. Whether functional use of drugs for such purposes is fully intentional or partially accidental, there can be no doubt that a proportion of drug problems originate in this way, as a result of self-medication.

3. Family Disruption

Drug dependence has been attributed to family problems, particularly early separation from one or both parents. Such persons experience a feeling of 'anomie'. They feel that there is hardly anyone to whom he/she is directly answerable. The inbuilt fear of the individual against the socially unacceptable behaviours diminishes slowly.

4. Lack of Communication in the Family

At family level, the most often cited factor is lack of healthy communication between the parents and the children. When the parents are themselves not clear what sort of values they cherish and honour, they usually find it extremely difficult to inculcate proper values in their children. From the beginning stress is laid upon honesty and truthfulness, while they themselves make so many compromises with these values. At an age when the children are initially exposed to the hypocrisy and double standards, they start feeling disillusioned and rebellious against authority. If the parents are unable to detect and handle this turmoil in their adolescent children, then these children become highly susceptible to use any such means which can relieve their frustration, boredom or loneliness. This relief is usually sought from anything in vogue whether it is "disco or drugs".

5. Predisposition

Evidence is emerging, particularly in the context of alcohol, that a genetic factor may be involved in some forms of drug abuse. What is actually inherited is so far less clear.

6. Availability

Availability, though is a very complex concept, yet embraces not only sheer physical availability, but also what can be called emotional availability, whether it is or is not 'all right' to take the drug. The fact that those who grow opium are prone to develop opium dependence or that doctors are apt to become dependent on their own drugs clearly shows the importance of this physical aspect of availability.

7. Personality Factors

Many authors have stated that a high proportion of institutionalized drug users have personality problems. Research results are in fact, somewhat contradictory and inconsistent. However, in relation to clinical population, opiate and heroin users do have disordered personalities. By and large, drug abusers are found to be lower in ego, strength and emotional stability, and higher in their state of anxiety and stress level.

8. Social and Economic Factors

Social scientists have interpreted drug abuse as partly a response to 'alienation'. People who are not well rewarded in the mainstream of society opt out and seek alternative gratifications from such things as drugs. More generally, such theories suggest that, even if drug use is not a response to educational failure or economic deprivation, it may be engendered by other social pressures and changes. The latter, it is argued, are not confined to the poor. There can be no doubt that in societies or sections of society where the ordinary social fabric has been disrupted by poverty, migration or rapid socio-economic change, are where the problems of drugs flourish. Another sociological theory of interest is that the punitive response to illegal drug use makes drug users become even more isolated and deviant. This may explain the difficulty of detaching chronic drug users from their adopted lifestyles. It does not, however, account for initial drug use. It is also clear that the production (and hence the use) of drugs may at times be deeply embedded in the economic life of a community, and even of an entire country. For example, cocaine production in certain countries of South America and opium production in certain Asian countries.

9. Curiosity

Popular wisdom usually sees drug problems as youth's problems and in many countries that may, to some extent, be legitimate. Youth is a time of experimentation, often including experimentation with drugs. It is the youth's curiosity that tempts her/him to experiment or to try anything new.

10. Sexual Identity

Some forms of drug abuse appear to be more common among males than females. It is not clear why this should be so. Social pressures, conventions and opportunities are possibly responsible for this pattern. In many societies, boys and young men are expected to be more daring, risk-taking, and rule-breaking than girls and young women. However, the finding that in many countries the prevalence of abuse of benzodiazepine is more among women than men indicates the unreliability of this stereotype explanation. It seems safe only to conclude that 'male-role' and 'female-role' can influence the drug taking behaviour in different ways, in different sociocultural settings.

The phenomenon of drug dependence, thus, has its roots in an individual's psychological, physical and environmental bases. Drugs are not addictive when they serve as a means of fulfilling a larger purpose in life, such as increased self-awareness, expanding consciousness or just plain enjoyment. But drugs are addictive when they are taken in order to hide from life, or to remain untouched by social order, and they become the sole source of gratification for that person who has chosen not to 'grow' and to control his or her own destiny. The use of any drug involves risks. The choice of risk depends on the cost versus worth equation constructed by an individual. The elements that must be considered are the drug, the individual, and the sociocultural milieu.

During childhood, behaviour is basically under the unchallenged control of parents and, to a lesser extent, of teachers and other adults who are in temporary contact with the child. During adolescence two new determinants of behaviour appear which are important in the context of drug use. One is the increasing importance of peers as role models, not the parents. The second is a tendency to take risks and to challenge established rules and values. In combination, these two sets of determinants of behaviour can lead to groups of adolescents taking risks or challenging established rules by a behaviour which none of the group would be likely to show alone or where none of the participants has had previous experience with the behaviour concerned. For example, initiation into group violence, alcohol intoxication or into taking of illicit drugs. These behaviours may exemplify the emotional and behavioural transitions accompanying puberty and the process of establishing one's individuality or individual personality.

It has been recorded that a career of drug-taking begins with an offer to take the drug. This offer, when successful, normally happens in circumstances where it is difficult to turn the offer down, in a situation which tends to be described, not very aptly, as social pressure or curiosity. More often it is in a situation which could probably best be described as conducive to impetuous or precipitous behaviour: a mixture of peer modelling, risk-taking and challenging prescribed rules of behaviour. It will simply be an offer of the opportunity to join with others in what appears to be a method of extending pleasurable aspects of conventional recreational situation. So in spite of being 'anti-drug', he or she evaluates the offer not in terms of drug-education but in terms of the current situation and the normal rules of behaviour (sociability, enjoyment, reciprocity, presenting self, etc.) appropriate in such recreational situations. This is true both for early offers of legal drugs (cigarettes and alcohol) and for later offers of illegal drugs (opium, heroin, etc.)

It has been argued that drug users who want to stop the drug taking-behaviour, go through a predictable sequence of different stages in which their motivation develops and changes. An individual seeking change, goes through four stages, namely, precontemplation, contemplation, action and maintenance. Precontemplators are those, who are not motivated to leave drugs. The task of the therapists is to motivate them to seek treatment. During the contemplation stage further motivational work is done by helping the drug-dependent to arrive at his/her own definition of the problem and the degree of damage done. Once the decision to change the drug-behaviour has been made, it is appropriate to embark upon behavioural and environmental change interventions. During this third stage (action), the drug-dependent is made to think more about 'how' to bring about change in his/her behaviour. Maintenance is a state in which a change in the behaviour is consolidated, and from which the individual may exit the cycle of change to a drug-free life, or the one where control over the behaviour becomes the norm.

Models of Drug Abuse

There are four major models of drug abuse and drug dependence, and each has a bias. None by itself provides a complete understanding of the world of substance abuse and dependence. These four models are: (a) the moral-legal model;

(b) the disease or public health model; (c) the psycho-social model; and (d) the sociocultural model. The major difference between the moral-legal and the disease or public health model is that the latter dwells less on the legality of the substance, and more on its potential harm. These two models operate from the premise that the answer to substance abuse problems is to keep substances away from the users. The psycho-social model and the sociocultural model take a different stand. These two models operate from the premise that the objective is to keep the persons away from addictive substances. The psycho-social model tends to put major emphasis on the individual rather than on the substance as the active agent. This model makes important distinctions among different use patterns, attitudes, and behaviours. But the sociocultural model views substance use and the problems associated with substance abuse from the social context, emphasizing environmental and socio-economic conditions.

Without getting confused with various models and approaches, one can accept the following description given by the World Health Organization (1980) as the starting point for our understanding of the problem of substance dependence : "Substance dependence is a state of periodic or chronic intoxication detrimental to the individual and to society produced by the repeated consumption of a substance (natural or synthetic). Its characteristics include: (a) an overpowering desire or need to continue taking the substance and to obtain it by any means; (b) a tendency to increase the dose; and (c) a psychic and sometimes a physical dependence on the effect of the substance". This eclectic approach assumes that the phenomenon of substance abuse and dependence is a product of a complex interaction among three variables namely: (a) the individual, (b) the substance, and (c) the environment. In other words, one can say that the substance effects are a function of interaction between the substance and the individual's physical, psychological, and social milieus.

A Psychological Study

The present research was an attempt to study drug abuse among the students with reference to some psycho-social concomitants. The objectives were to compare : (i) the frustration level and the modes of frustration of drug abusers and non-abusers: and also (ii) to study both the groups in terms of their self-esteem.

Frustration is a state when an individual is prevented by some obstacle from reaching a goal and which may lead to an aggressive behaviour. It is also hypothesized that higher degree of frustration may lead to drug abuse. The self-esteem on the other hand is concerned with self-respect, self-confidence, a feeling of personal worth and recognition. Satisfaction of these needs produces feelings of prestige, power and control. Esteem need not always be obtained through mature or adaptive behaviour. It is sometimes generated by disruptive and irresponsible actions also.

The two hypotheses framed in this study are :

(i) Drug abusers and non-abusers have different levels of frustration.

(ii) Drug abusers and non-abusers differ in terms of their self-esteem need.

Methodology

Sample

Total sample consisted of two hundred students comprising drug abusers (N=100) and non-drug abusers (N=100). Drug abuser group was identified after making a survey of 1600 students. Out of these one hundred drug-abusers and one hundred non-abusers were taken for the present study. Both the groups were matched in terms of age, education and socio-economic status. The subjects' age range was 18-28 yrs.

Tools used :

The tools used for the present study were :

(i) Self-esteem inventory (ii) Frustration test.

Self-esteem inventory

Self-esteem inventory has been devised by *Prasad and Thakur (1977)*. They argued that self-esteem ('personally perceived self' and 'socially perceived self') constitute the whole self of the individual.

The test comprises of two identical sets of 30 items with different instructions for each set. The instructions given to the subjects are as follows :

There are some statements in this inventory. Please read these statements one by one carefully. Each statement has seven point rating scale from completely true to completely false. You have to encircle the point of the scale related to the particular statement which in your personal opinion is most suitable.

This instruction was given for the first set. For the second set the instructions were : Again you are given the same set of statements which you rated earlier on the basis of your personal opinion. This time, however, you have to rate on the basis of your idea about what others think of you.

Scoring and Interpretation : In the self-esteem test, there are thirty items in which 17 are socially desirable and 13 are socially undesirable. All the items were rated on 7 point scale, which run from completely true to completely false. Socially undesirable items are scored negatively, i.e. the completely false point would get 7 scores and completely true would get 1 score. An individual who has taken both the sets of the inventory will have scores—one for the 'personally perceived self' and the other for the 'socially perceived self.'

If personally perceived score is higher than the socially perceived score, the person has positive self. If socially perceived score is higher than the personally perceived score the person has negative self, and if persons get identical scores on both the sets, they are termed as persons with balanced self-esteem.

Frustration test

Frustration test has been devised by *Chauhan and Tiwari (1972)*. The scale consists of 40 items which comprise of four dimensions of frustration, i.e. regression, fixation, resignation and aggression. Each dimension has 10 items.

The instructions given to the drug-abusers and non-abusers are as follows : There are questions each having five choices. Select one answer which seems to be more appropriate to you and tick in the side parenthesis. Answer all the questions.

The answers given by the subjects were converted into scores for analytical purposes, for all the four dimensions of frustration.

The biographical information regarding the subjects were also taken which included age, sex, education, family size, family income, marital status, religion and drugs used/not used. An information blank was prepared for this purpose. The tests along with the biographical information blank were given to the drug abusers and the non-abusers and data were collected.

Scoring Procedure

Self-esteem inventory : Scoring for both personally perceived self and socially perceived self were done for both the groups of subjects and were subjected to analysis.

Frustration test : Scores for four different dimensions of frustration of both the groups were also calculated as per manual instruction.

Results

Self-esteem test

The self-esteem inventory has two parts, "personally perceived self", and other "socially perceived self". Scoring of both the sets was done separately. Tables 14.1 and 14.2 present the results of the t-Test for the two groups of subjects.

TABLE 14.1

't' Value for the Two Groups of Subjects on "Personally Perceived Self"

Group	*N*	*Mean*	*S.D.*	*t-value*
Drug abuser	100	141.54	13.63	0.29 N.S.
Non-abuser	100	140.86	18.72	

Table 14.1 shows that 't' value is insignificant. Hence these two groups did not differ significantly with respect to personally perceived self scores.

TABLE 14.2

't' Value for the Two Groups of Subjects on "Socially Perceived Self"

Group	*N*	*Mean*	*S.D.*	*t-value*
Drug abuser	100	136.02	16.93	0.85 N.S.
Non-abuser	100	138.04	16.84	

Table 14.2 also reveals that the drug abusers and non-abusers do not differ with respect to socially perceived self as 't' value was insignificant.

Frustration Test

Scores for the four dimensions of frustration were compared by t-test between the two groups. The results are presented in Tables 14.3 to 14.6.

TABLE 14.3

'T' Value for the Two Groups of Subjects on "Regression".

Group	*N*	*Mean*	*S.D.*	*t-value*
Drug abuser	100	32.12	8.52	6.75*
Non-abuser	100	24.76	6.78	

*Significant at 0.01 level.

Table 14.3 shows the results of the 't' test for the two groups in respect of regression. Obtained 't' value (6.75) was highly significant at 0.01 level.

TABLE 14.4

't' Value for the Two Groups of Subjects on "Fixation"

Group	*N*	*Mean*	*S.D.*	*t-value*
Drug abuser	100	27.26	8.57	2.00*
Non-abuser	100	24.77	8.93	

*Significant at 0.05 level.

Table 14.4 shows the comparison of the two groups with respect to fixation. The obtained 't' -value (2.0) was significant at 0.05 level. Scores of drug abusers group were higher than the non-abusers group.

TABLE 14.5

't' Value for the Two Groups of Subjects on "Resignation".

Group	*N*	*Mean*	*S.D.*	*t-value*
Drug abuser	100	29.08	9.29	
				4.60*
Non-abuser	100	22.91	9.62	

*Significant at 0.01 level.

Table 14.5 shows that the two groups, i.e. drug abusers and non-abusers significantly differ with respect to resignation. t-value (4.60) was highly significant at 0.01 level. Higher scores of drug abusers group indicate the tendency towards resignation as a mode of frustration.

TABLE 14.6

't' Value for the Two Groups of Subjects on "Aggression"

Group	*N*	*Mean*	*S.D.*	*t-value*
Drug abuser	100	28.98	8.75	
				2.00*
Non-abuser	100	31.28	6.95	

* Significant at 0.05 level.

Table 14.6 shows that the obtained t-value (2.0) is significant at 0.5 level.

TABLE 14.7

Summary of the Results for the Two groups of Subjects on the Four Dimensions of Frustration Test.

Variable	*t-value*	*P.*
Regression	6.75	<.01
Fixation	2.00	<.05
Resignation	4.60	<.01
Aggression	2.00	<.05

Table 14.7 gives the summary of the results of the 't' test, for the two groups of subjects.

Discussion and Interpretation

In the present research an attempt was made to study some of the psycho-social variables in relation to drug abuse behaviour. The results showed that both the drug abuser and non-abuser groups have positive attitude on the self-esteem dimension of the personality. When compared the frustration level, drug abuser group is found to be more frustrated. From the Tables 14.1 and 14.2, it could be seen that "personally perceived self" and "socially perceived self" of self-esteem did not differ statistically in the two groups indicating that both the groups have clear self concept and a positive attitude towards self on the "socially perceived self" dimension. However, drug abuser group, scored lower than the non-abuser group. It can be pointed out that in both the groups "personally perceived self" scores are higher than the "socially perceived self" scores. The results of self-esteem, i.e. 'personally perceived self' and 'socially perceived self' for the two groups show that there is no significant difference between the groups. This may be due to the fact that both the groups are from student community and they are well aware about the consequences of drugs. But as far as drug abuse is concerned few students indulge in intoxication regularly. A large number of students have been found to have taken drugs occasionally, e.g. in ritual ceremonies, marriage parties and they are all from good family backgrounds. The scores of self-esteem, therefore, in the two groups were similar.

So far as the frustration test is concerned the drug abuser group fell in the high frustration category (Table 14.3), whereas non-abuser group fell in the average frustration category.

It is pertinent to mention here that both the groups of subjects fall in the average frustration category on 'fixation' but they differ at 0.05 level. The drug abuser group scored little higher than the non-abuser group on fixation score. On the 'resignation' dimension the drug abusers group scored higher than the non-abuser group. They also scored higher on regression dimension. 'Aggression' as a mode of frustration also significantly differ at 0.05 level, meaning thereby that non-abuser group is more aggressive than their counterparts, i.e. the drug abuser group. The significantly higher scores of drug abuser group on the three out of four modes of frustration, i.e. regression, fixation, aggression and resignation are indicative of higher frustration level.

This result can be explained in relation to a study of *Barry (1974)*. He mentioned that the functional significance of drug abuser lies in the ability to maintain and enhance regression. There is a tendency of drug abusers (while intoxicated) to express impulsively their dominant mood or emotion while simultaneously suppressing incompatible motives.

In the present study the results show that regression, fixation and resignation as the modes of frustration are dominant among drug abusers. High frustration among the drug abusers have been shown by other researchers also. For example, *McClelland and his associates (1972)*, believe that alcoholism is a result of frustrated ambitions and a consequent fall from status. The drug abuser is pictured as having an enhanced need for power but inadequate personality resources to achieve the goal. In the face of frustrated ambitions the abuser resorts to drugs to achieve a euphoric sense of power and achievement, as well as a release from tension. *Biancon (1986)* also found that the subjects of his study had personalities based on frustration and lack of social interest and antisocial attitude. *Hendiri and Hass (1985)* examined drug taking and related behaviour in the context of psycho-social adaptation. They found that chronic use was related to adaptive difficulties derived in a major part from troubled family relationships and conflict over competition and aggression. For adolescents, chronic use was associated with deviance or provocation directed at authority, reinforcement of fantasy and assistance in withdrawal from competition/achievement conflict. Chronic usage was also observed to be related to a general break with parental and social values, and also anger and frustration produced by unhappy relationships.

It is useful here to throw some light on some of the observations made by the present investigators during the study. It has been observed that all the students among the abusers and non-abusers belong to good family background. They are economically balanced. Their fathers are working either in government or private service. As far as drug abuser is concerned, it can be pointed out that to fulfil the higher demands of the society, to maintain dignity in society, to increase the family income for catering their needs, generally parents and other family members are more anxious and frustrated.

It was also observed that on most of the variables, drug abuser groups did not differ from non-abuser groups on "socially perceived self" and "personally perceived self" (Tables 14.1 & 14.2). This could be explained in a way that the students perhaps get healthy attention and have better interaction with their parents as well as with other family members. Drugs have their effects on the body as well as on the mind. Efficiency of a person who becomes a drug addict is drastically reduced. His relationship with his family members relatives, friends and all other members of the society, becomes thin and indifferent. Drug dependency also affects the lifestyle and the personality of the drug dependent person, specially the students, who are emotionally immature and rigid to new ideas. They have high level of frustration, anxiety and depression. They are either jovial and loving, or angry and hostile. But they do not know why they feel as they do.

Conclusions

In the context of the results and interpretations the conclusions drawn may be summed up as follows :

1. The present study was carried out among the students of Delhi University on a problem entitled "Prevalence of Drug Abuse among Delhi University Students : A Study of Some Psycho-Social Concomitants".
2. After identifying the drug abuser group of students in the first phase of the survey two psychological tests (i.e., self-esteem test and frustration test) were administered on both the groups of drug abusers (N=100) and non-abusers (N=100). On the basis of the study it was found that the two groups of students namely, drug abusers and non-abusers differed in some aspects :
   - (i) There is a significant difference between the drug abuser group and non-abuser group in terms of their psycho-social concomitants.
   - (ii) Both the groups of drug abuser and non-abuser seem to have high self-esteem and positive self. When both the groups were compared on the dimension of self-esteem test (i.e., 'personally perceived self' and 'socially perceived self') they were found to be similar.
   - (iii) Drug abuser groups are found to be more frustrated in comparison to non-abuser groups. Three modes (regression, fixation, resignation) of frustration are more prevalent among the drug abusers.

Suggestions

Drug abuse is more a social problem than a reflection of personal inadequacy. Our culture encourages the use of drugs in a variety of situations and the restrictive (though partial) prohibitions imposed in the country appear to encourage rather than reduce, the magnitude of drug abuse.

The findings of the present investigation lack generality because the study is conducted only on those students who are studying at Delhi University. Therefore, it is a need of the times that such studies must be carried out on varied and larger samples. Further researches regarding the prevalence of drug abuse in relation to psycho-social factors should be carried out in-depth.

There are three aspects namely, prevention, treatment and rehabilitation of drug addicts. The result of this study could be utilized for understanding the cause of the problem, prevention and treatment of drug-addict students. For any psychotherapist or psychiatrist the results of the study can help in deciding the line of intervention strategies. Parents, doctors, teachers, sociologists, psychologists and the society as such can be of great help in preventing and controlling the problem of drug abuse by understanding the various psycho-social factors which could precipitate the problem.

15

CONCLUSION

The present study was designed to study the prevalence of drug abuse among Delhi University students and its relation to some psycho-social concomitants.

To secure information regarding drug abuse, especially from students' community, was a difficult job. It was planned to contact personally by keeping them in confidence. In all 1600 students from different professional and non-professional colleges of Delhi University were contacted. To seek information regarding drug abuse, a structured questionnaire was given to each subject. They were convinced that information provided by them will be kept strictly confidential.

On collecting data from 1600 students, it was found that 620 (38.75%) students admitted to having taken drugs, in which tobacco has the highest prevalence rate, i.e. 19.56%. Others are as follows: alcohol (11.69%), opiates (0.69%), cannabis (0.69%), tranquillizers (2.38%), amphetamines (0.88%), barbiturates (0.38%), sedatives (0.38%). It was also found that the combination of use of tobacco followed by alcohol (1.63%), cigarette followed by cannabis (0.31%), cigarette followed by tranquillizers (0.63%), cigarette followed by amphetamine (0.63%) and cigarette followed by alcohol and cannabis (0.63%) was widespread.

After having the information from drug users and non-users, the drug abusers were compared with non-abusers in terms of their types of family (nuclear and joint), occupation of father and their family income (Tables 12.6 and 12.7). Moreover, drug abusers were also compared with non-abusers in terms of their physical and mental health (Tables 12.9 and 12.10).

All the abovementioned aspects pertaining to drug abuse were found to be significant between users and non-users. It is pointed out that drug has its effects on the body as well as on the mind. Efficiency of a person who becomes a drug addict is drastically reduced. His mental and physical capabilities are adversely affected resulting in poor performance at work. His relationship with his family members, relatives, friends and all other members of the society, becomes poor and indifferent. On account of financial constraints, an addict may also not be in a position to afford the drugs with his limited income. He may start indulging in malpractices and may also go to the extent of committing serious crimes. Since, it is a progressive disease, it can be chronic and fatal, if not treated and arrested at the right time. It was also observed from the sample that no student wants to develop 'dependency'. Even those who decide to experiment with drugs, do so only with the attitude that "it will never happen to me". But there is, still, a systematic progression towards drugs dependency affecting the lifestyle and the personality of the drug dependent person. Specially the student is emotionally immature and rigid to new ideas. He has high level of frustration, anxiety and depression. He is either jovial and loving, or angry and hostile. But he does not know why he feels as he does. It is also important to mention that non-medical drug use produces alteration in consciousness of the user. Perceptual and cognitive nature changes the user's mood, performance and state of well-being. It is useful to mention that a few students reported that they have taken dependence-producing drugs on few occasions. They were motivated by curiosity, peer pressure, pleasure and removal of anxiety.

The results of the present study can be summarized as follows:

(i) Prevalence of drug abuse was found to be different in different groups of students namely, general, medical, and engineering (Table 12.1).

(ii) Drug abusers group differs with the variation of their frequency in terms of intake of hard drugs and also soft drugs. Table 12.2 shows the frequency and percentage rate of using hard and soft drugs by students of all disciplines. On the basis of the pattern of the results, it can be concluded that 'irrespective of the students' course discipline the use of different types of drugs is similar.

(iii) Drug abusers differ from the non-abusers group in terms of their background variables, viz., types of family, occupation of the father and family income (Tables 12.6 and 12.7).

(iv) There is a difference between the drug abuser group and non-abuser group in terms of their physical and mental health (Tables 12.9 and 12.10).

(v) Drug abuser group is more anxious and frustrated than that of the non-abuser group.

There are three aspects namely, prevention, treatment and rehabilitation of drug addicts. The result of this study can be utilized for understanding the cause of the problem, prevention and treatment of drug-addict students. For any psychotherapist or psychiatrist the results of the study can help in deciding the line of intervention strategies. Parents, doctors, teachers, sociologists, psychologists and the society as such can be of great help in preventing and controlling the problem of drug abuse by understanding the various psycho-social factors which could precipitate the problem.

By giving adequate attention, the problem of drug abuse can be prevented and controlled. The Ministry of Welfare has evolved a comprehensive policy for mobilizing voluntary action to create an awareness and consciousness for the prevention of drug abuse. A large number of voluntary organizations are being supported to educate the people about the ill effects of drug addiction. It has also funded the establishment of counselling and deaddiction facilities. With a view to provide a special focus on the youth, the State Government/Union Territory Administration have been advised to impress upon the University authorities to mount a special vigil against liquor drinking and drug abuse in educational campuses/ hostels.

There are several other professional groups like psychologists, counsellers, educators, etc, who are directly or indirectly concerned with alcoholism and drug abuse. Among these, teachers and academicians can play an important role in the prevention of drug abuse among student groups. The preventive strategies against drug abuse accord a high priority to safeguarding the young persons in academic institutions. In this regard, it may be pointed out that a variety of training techniques such as workshops, discussions, role playing, decision-making and problem-solving exercises and other allied activities are being universally stressed. Through the training of teachers, the prevention of drug abuse in educational institutions can be achieved, for the ultimate welfare of the student community.

It is also suggested that community based agencies including educational, religious and social welfare organizations can play a crucial role in regard to the identification, referral and mobilization of rehabilitative resources.

It is obvious that the medical treatment of drug addicts is the responsibility of the medical profession. The preventive aspect entails contribution by diverse groups engaged in law enforcement, education, health, social welfare, mass media, etc. Moreover, the general public has to be made aware of the ill-effects of drug abuse on the individual, the family and the society. A comprehensive strategy in this regard would naturally involve the induction of drug education component in professional curricula of various disciplines as well as a well-rounded programme of orientation and refresher courses for different groups concerned with the problems.

Drug abuse is more a social problem than a reflection of personal inadequacy. Our culture encourages the use of drugs in a variety of situations and the restrictive (though partial) prohibitions imposed in the country appear to encourage rather than reduce, the magnitude of drug abuse. The distinction between licit and illicit drugs is likewise arbitrary and the line between drug use and abuse has yet to be rationally defended. It is observed that drugs with comparable side effects are outlawed while alcohol and nicotine (cigarettes, etc,) are openly marketed. It raises a question whether the drug laws are consistent in their alleged protection of the physical health and mental well-being of the individuals and the society.

An Overview

The world is facing a global threat to health of rapidly worsening dimensions. It is clear that based on current trends the number of drug abusers are escalating both in countries where there has been a long history of problems as well as countries which were previously relatively free from drug abuse. Although the problem of drug abuse is not a new phenomenon, it has effected different cultures and societies on many occasions earlier also. There are also examples of effective measures taken by the societies then. The problem of drug abuse has not only multiplied in quantum but has also become complicated and multifaceted. Earlier the choice of drug for a particular community was determined by the geographical habitats, the nature of community life, the historical era, the availability of drug and the occasion of use. Hence different communities had different drugs at different times for their different purposes in the various parts of the world. In recent time, there is a change in the trends in drug abuse. Natural drugs such as cannabis, cocaine, khat and opium which were previously being used within certain cultural settings and confined to a particular geographical area are now being exposed in other regions also. Easy availability of manufactured drugs such as amphetamines, barbiturates, sedatives and tranquillizers have further complicated the problem of drug abuse. Earlier drugs were primarily used by adults. Now, all types of dependence producing drugs are being abused by preadolescents and adolescents. Multiple drug use is another feature of new trends of drug abuse. Since 1980s, the international drug scenario has changed dramatically. The use of illicit drugs such as heroin and cocaine has increased by a factor of 10 and there has been increase in the harmful use of licit drugs and alcohol especially in developing countries *(WHO, 1993)*.

Another problem with international drug abuse situation is global cultivation and production of opium, coca and cannabis which continues to expand. The supply of the products made from these crops far exceeds the demand for them. But the demand is also rising particularly in the producing and trafficking countries. These countries once immune from the effects of illicit drugs, now have growing addicts and abusing population. Drug production and trafficking are a big business. The product is lucrative, needs little advertising and keeps the customer coming back for more. The criminal organizations running this business are skillful and ruthless. They fight back against all organized efforts to curtail their activities. Frequent change in their target areas keeps their business running. Sophisticated control measures introduced by industrialized countries which constituted the principle market in illicit drugs have prompted the traffickers to locate laboratories for production of both cocaine and heroin in the developing countries that provide the raw material. The availability of refined drugs of high purity and at low prices has expanded the markets for these drugs in these and neighbouring countries. Drastic developments in transportation, migration and communication have further facilitated the smuggling of illicit commodities. Advancement in transportation has also brought people in easy contact with each other's customs and behaviour, thus enabling people to experiment with psychoactive drugs that might not be available at home. The greatest increase in cross cultural contact has been through the growth in long distance communication in particular, by means of the electronic media. Television programmes about hi-fi societies build desires for often unattainable lifestyles. Drinking and drug use often portray a symbol of high society. This influences the viewers to indulge in cigarette smoking, alcohol consumption and consumption of drugs. With respect to illicit drugs the overall picture is of enormous growth in world supply which has affected developing and developed countries alike. Many countries that originally were consumers of licit psychoactive medicinal drugs are now also producers of these drugs.

In India there has been a sharp rise in drug abuse especially of heroin since past decade and-a-half. Various evidences have revealed easy availability of this drug in India. One of the major factors that has lead to easy availability is 'Spill over effect' of excessive availability in neighbouring countries. India has turned into a transit country between the two major sources of illicit drugs in the world the 'Golden Triangle' (comprising of Myanmar, Thailand and Laos and the 'Golden Crescent' (comprising Pakistan, Afghanistan and Iran) to its destination in the West. Thus, over the years from being a transit country India has also turned into a consumer country of drugs.

Contemporary situation in drug abuse has one thing in common that it is universally prevalent. The magnitude of the problem may vary from country to country but there is a significant rise in the prevalence of drug abuse in the world.

The last decade has seen the emergence and rise of another fatal disease associated with drug abuse, i.e. HIV (Human Immuno-deficiency Virus). The use of psychoactive drugs has facilitated the spread of HIV infection in several ways. The most direct way is by transmission of HIV through needles shared by intravenous drug abusers. Another common mode of HIV transmission is through sexual contacts. Many drug abusers have engaged in prostitution in order to enable them to purchase psychoactive drugs. Alcohol and other psychoactive drugs are regarded as disinhibitors and under their influence many engage in sexual and other high risk behaviours that they might otherwise avoid. Some psychoactive drugs may also hasten the onset of Acquired Immuno Deficiency Syndrome (AIDS) by depressing immune function. Intravenous drug abusers are a high risk group to HIV infection and are the second largest group infected with HIV. According to *WHO (1993)* the prevalence of HIV infection among intravenous drug abusers is up to 58% in France, 20% in Germany, 30-80% in Italy, 30% in the Netherlands, 40-60% in Spain and 1-5% in the United Kingdom. Reports from South America, India and Thailand indicate that the infection is spreading rapidly among certain group of injecting drug abusers and among some non injecting drug abusers. The factors that appear to be primarily responsible for the rapid spread of HIV among drug abusers are :

(i) Lack of awareness about AIDS (ii) Sexual contact (iii) Sharing of needle and syringes at sites frequented by drug users.

In a recent report of Government of India, the HIV/AIDS spread through injecting needles is as high as 6.5%. Highest incidence of HIV has been reported in Manipur, Maharashtra and Tamil Nadu *(NACO, 1993)*. According to *NACO (1994)* prevalence of HIV in intravenous drug abusers in Manipur is 55.76% and percentage of injecting drug abusers in Manipur, Mizoram and Nagaland is 1% to 2% of total population in a state *(NICED, 1992)*. According to U.S. Bureau of Census, 1991, the prevalence of HIV amongst intravenous drug users is 38.40%.

Another problem associated with drug abuse is crime, violence and other illegal activities. Alcohol is the commonest drug which is associated with a variety of violent behaviours, sexual assault, suicide, criminal homicide, violence within family and road accidents *(Sharma, 1993)*. Besides the provocation of aggressive behaviour, the intense desire for drug prompts the person to indulge in antisocial activities like stealing at home, stealing outside, drug peddling and other criminal activities which will facilitate them to purchase the drug and fulfil their needs. Drug trafficking in the nineties has opened a new chapter on violence in India. The narco terrorism link and its security implications at the state level (especially in Punjab, Jammu-Kashmir and Tamil Nadu) and at national level often appear as headlines in the print media *(Sharma, 1993)*. In recent years, drugs have emerged as ideal commodities for organized crime across national boundries. The operators of these organized crimes are well disciplined but confrontation with law enforcement agencies and street level violence in peddling of illicit drugs are frequent *(Sharma, 1993)*.

Steps to Control Drug Abuse

The multifaceted problem of drug abuse has no one line solution to it. This has to be dealt with from various angles. A number of steps are simultaneously required to combat drug abuse. The different steps needed to control drug abuse problem may be as follows:

1. Supply Reduction

The problem of drug abuse is multiplied because of easy availability of the drugs. Control in the availability will definitely bring down the number of present drug abusers and future drug abusers prone to it. To induce the supply reduction, efforts have to be made to control the entry of drugs from various possible sources. Strict checks at the national borders especially where the political relations are not in good tune are required to stop the easy entry of drugs in the country. Controlling cultivation as close to the source as possible is the most efficient and cost effective means of reducing the supply of illicit drugs. There are several approaches including eradication, crop substitution and area targeted development. Arial spraying of herbicide is an effective mode to control illicit cultivation of cannabis and opium poppy plants.

2. Demand Reduction

Without addressing the demand side of drug problem, efforts to reduce supplies are ineffective. Reducing demand is an important key to contain the problem. The components of the drug reduction strategy are: (i) awareness building and educating people about the ill effects of drug abuse; (ii) community based action for the identification, treatment and rehabilitation of drug addicts; (iii) training of professionals and nonprofessionals engaged in drug abuse prevention, treatment and control.

3. Public Awareness and Prevention Programmes

These programmes can be quite effective in creating a climate for discouraging illicit drug abuse and can alert potential abusers to the dangers of illicit drug abuse before they become embroiled in it. Such awareness programmes can not only prevent potential drug abusers but would also motivate abusers to approach health agencies for treatment and rehabilitation. Family and society on the whole can be informed through such programmes about the expected behaviour from them. In India, 217 centres are working to build awareness and give assistance and counselling to abusers and their families.

4. Treatment and Rehabilitation

Health agencies all over the world are working diligently to determine how illegal drugs affect people — physically and psychologically and what types of treatment programmes can most effectively help drug dependent individuals to overcome their problems. In India 121 centres are working all over the country to facilitate deaddiction and rehabilitation of the addicts.

Research is the only way to understand the magnitude of the problem, its cause, factors associated with it and the pattern of drug abuse. Good prevalence data are a prerequisite for designing and implementing an effective demand reduction programme. Only research can identify the precipitating factors which lead to drug abuse and treatment programmes to help drug abusers to overcome the problem.

5. Legal and Alternative Drug Control Measures

Legal measures that can be directed against traffickers include disrupting the processing and transportation systems and employing stringent enforcement measures such as arrest, extradition and seizure of assets. The amended Narcotic Drugs and Psychotropic Substance Act, 1988 and the Prevention of Illicit Traffic in Narcotic Drugs and Psychotropic Substance Act, 1988 are two recent laws of the Government of India to contain the problem legally. In these Acts, provisions have been made for control and regulation of operations related to narcotic drugs and psychotropic substances. Under this Act, no person can produce or manufacture, possess, sell, purchase, export and import interstate narcotic drugs and psychotropic substances except for scientific and medicinal purposes. Stringent penal provisions are provided for in case of violation.

Future Prospects

From the changing trends in drug abuse, it appears that the problem of drug abuse is on the rise. It has universally struck the adolescents and preadolescents. The health, social and economic implications of drug abuse are many. They vary from big business for the producers and drug traffickers to unemployment and lack of meaningful goal for the drug abusers. Serious health problems vary from AIDS, road accidents, to diseases like cirrhosis of liver and tuberculosis. Indulgence of youth in drug abuse is an economic loss not only to the family and society but also to the country as a whole. Laundering money available with the drug traffickers and others involved in a similar kind of business facilitates antisocial activities in the societies and countries. Lots of governmental money is being spent to control, treat and rehabilitate drug abusers which could very well be utilized for some other developmental programme. This is again a financial loss to the country.

The problem of drug abuse can only be controlled by sincerely checking the production and trafficking of the drugs, bringing about intensified public awareness and implementing prevention programmes. The treatment and rehabilitation of those already in drug abuse is an essential component of control measures. A constant eye on the prevalence rate and other related factors through different monitoring systems is important to estimate the problem from time to time. Networking within the country and at international level will help in viewing the problem at a broader level. The situation is serious but not hopeless. Although the evidences show that the drug abuse is increasing but good models of preventing drug problems can also be traced in history.

APPENDIX 1

Drug Abuse Survey Questionnaire for Students

Name and address (Optional) :

Name of the college :

Age : Sex : Male/Female

Religion :

Marital status : Married/Unmarried

Size of the family :

Educational qualifications :

Percentage of marks obtained in the previous examination :

Total family income per month :

0-2000	2000-4000	4000-6000	6000-8000
8000-10000	10000-12000	12000-14000	14000-16000
16000-18000	18000-20000	20000 and above	

Parent's occupation : Father : Mother

Was any member of your family taking drugs? Yes/No

If yes, what is your relationship with the member?

Do you take any drug? Yes/No

If you are taking any of the following drug(s), then answer the following :

Type of Drug Used	*Age of First Use*	*Age of Regular Use*	*Frequency*	*Mode of use Smoking/ Injecting/ Drinking*
Bidi				
Cigarette				
Hukka				
Smack				
Alcohol				
Opiates				

Barbiturates			
Opium			
Heroin			
Cannabis			
Tranqui-llizers			
Amphet-amines			
Sedatives			
Others			

Give reasons of your drug use : Peer pressure/curiosity/for pleasure/to remove anxiety/initial free supply of drugs/others (please specify).

When you took the drug for the first time, mention the source of procurement:

General sources : Single/Multiple; street peddler; tea/pan shop; friend; any other (please specify).

Where do you take drugs frequently? College, college hostel, bar, road-sides, hotels, home, any other place (specify).

What do you understand by drug abuse?

What do you feel are the consequences of drug abuse?

Do you think it is possible to stop taking drugs? Yes/No

If yes, then who can help you to stop?

How do you rate your mental and physical health as compared to others of your age? Excellent/good/average/poor/very poor

BIBLIOGRAPHY

Abed, R.T., Neira-Munoz, E. (1990) A survey of general practitioners' opinion and attitude to drug addicts and addiction. *British Journal of Addiction,* 85: 131-136.

Abelson, P.H. (1970) Death from Heroin. *Science,* 168: 1289.

Adityanjee, Mohan, D. and Saxena, S. (1984) Heroin Dependence— The New Delhi Experience. *The Indian Journal of Psychiatry,* 26: 312-16.

Ahmad, Anis, Sen, A.K. and Chadha, N.K. (1995) Prevalence of Drug-abuse among Aligarh Muslim University Students: A Survey Report, *Disabilities and Impairments,* 9: 85-95.

Ahuja, R. (1986) Research in Drug Abuse : An Overview. National Seminar on Drug Abuse, National Institute of Public Cooperation and Child Development, New Delhi, 29-30 September.

Alistair, M.G. (1985) Psycho-social Aspect of Drug Abuse, *Recent Advances in Clinical Psychiatry* (5).

American Psychiatric Association (1974) Position Statement on Barbiturates, *American Journal of Psychiatry,* 131 (6), 743.

Andrews, H.L. (1941) Brain Potentials and Morphine Addiction. *Psychosomatic Medicine,* 3:399-409.

——— **(1943)** The Effects of Opiates on the Pain Threshold in Post-addicts. *Journal of Clinical Investigation,* 22: 511-516.

Armstrong, J.D. (1958) The Search for the Alcoholic Personality. *Annals of the American Academy of Political and Social Science,* 315: 40-47.

Arneja, I. and Sen, A.K. (1982a) Personality Characteristics of Drug Abusers and Non-Abusers : A Factor Analytic Study. *Disabilities and Impairments,* 2: 9-22.

————, **(1982b)** A Comparative Study of Drug Abusers and Non Abusers in Some Psycho-social Variables. *Disabilities and Impairments,* 3: 104-116

————, **(1990)** Prevalence of Drug Abuse among Delhi University Students— A Survey Report, *Disabilities and Impairments,* 3: 99-107.

Bacon, Selden D. (1945) Alcohol and Complex Society: 179-200 *Quarterly Journal of Studies on Alcohol* in Yale University, Laboratory of Applied Psychology, School of Alcohol Studies, Alcohol; Science and Society, New Haven.

Bagadia, V.N, Jethi, G., Pradhan, P.N. and Shah, L.P. (1976) Habitual Use of Cannabis in Psychiatric Patients— A deep study of 20 cases. *Indian Journal of Psychiatry,* 18, 141.

Ball, J.C. & Ross, A. (1991) *The Effectiveness of Methadone Treatment : Patients, Programmes, Services, and Outcome.* New York : Springerverlang.

Banerjee, D. (1989) Drug Abuse : Its magnitude. Paper presented at the National Seminar held at Miranda House, Delhi University, from February 16-18.

Banerjee, R.N. (1963) Prevalence of Habit Forming Drugs and Smoking among College Students— A Survey. *Indian Medical Journal,* 57, 193.

Barry, H. (1974) Psychological Factors in Alcoholism. In B. Kissin and H. Begleiter (eds.), *The Biology of Alcoholism,* 3: 53-108 *Clinical Pathology*. New York : Plenum Publishing Corporation.

Basu, D.; Malhotra, A.; Verma, V.K., & Malhotra, R. (1997) Attitudes Towards Drug Taking Behaviour : A Factor Analytic Study. *Journal of the Indian Academy of Applied Psychology,* Vol. 23, No. 1-2: 23-29.

Bazell, R.J. (1973) Drug Abuse : Methadone Becomes the Solution and the Problem. *Science,* 179(4075): 772-75.

Bejerot, N. (1972) *Addiction : An Artificially Induced Drive,* Springfield, Illinois : Charles C. Thomas.

Bhadra, B.R., & Girija, P.R. (1981) Attitude, belief and behaviour toward alcohol use. In D. Mohan, H.S. Sethi and E. Tongue (eds.), *Current Research in Drug Abuse in India.* Delhi : Gemini Press.

Bhatia, P., Muhar, I.S. and Saroj. (1995) Maladjustment and Drug Abuse. *Disabilities and Impairments : An Interdisciplinary Research Journal,* 9.

Biacon, Silvia (1986) (Ospedale Psichiatrico S. Mariadella Piela, Ceccano, Italy) Anomie and Alcoholism : Contribution to the Sociopathological Study of Chronic Alcoholic Intoxication, *(Italy) havoro Neuropsichiatrico,* (1981), 67: 119-126.

Blachly, P.H. (1970) *Seduction : A Conceptual Model in the Drug Dependencies and Other Contagious ills.* Springfield, Illinois: Charles C. Thomas.

Boyd, P. (1970) Heroin Addiction in Adolescents. *Journal of Psychosomatic Research,* 14: 295-301.

Brook, J.S., Lukoff, I.F., & Whiteman, M. (1980) Initiation into adolescent marijuana use. *Journal of Genetic Psychology,* 137: 133-142.

Broota, K.D. and Singh, S. (1986) Adjustment Problems and Socio-personal Variables in Drug Abuse. *Indian Journal of Clinical Psychology,* 13(1), 59.

Brown, J.S. and Farber, I.E. (1951) Emotions Conceptualized as Intervening Variables with Suggestions towards a Theory of Frustration, *Psychological Bulletin,* 48: 465-80.

Brown, R.R. (1940) The Relation of Body Build to Drug Addiction. *Public Health Reports,* 55: 1954-63.

———, (1946) A Cyle of Morphine Addiction: Biological and Psychological Studies. Part-2 : Psychological Investigations. *Public Health Reports,* 61: 37-53.

Bullard, Dexter M.; Hoffman, Barbara R.; and Havens, Leston L. (1960). The Relative Value of Tranquilizing Drugs and Social and Psychological Therapies in chronic Schizophrenia. *Psychiatric Quarterly,* 34: 293-306.

Callaway, Enoch; and Stone, George C. (1960) Psychopharmacologic Theories : A Critical Review. *Clinical Pharmacology and Therapeutics,* 1:247-67.

Chakraborty, A.K.; Roy, M. & Ganguly, S.S. (1980) Drug Abuse in Medical Students in Calcutta— A Preliminary Study. *Indian Journal of Medical Research,* 71: 465.

Chappel, J.N. & Schnoll, S. (1977) Physician attitudes : Effects on the treatment of Chemically dependent patients. *Journal of American Medical Association*, 237: 2318-319.

Chauhan, N.S. and Tiwari, G. (1972) Frustration-Test. Published by Agra Psychological Research Cell, Agra (India).

Chein, Isidor et al. (1964) *The Road to H : Narcotics, Delinquency and Social Policy.* New York : Basic Books (Part-I describes a comprehensive programme of research on adolescent drug use.)

Chein, I. (1966) Psychological, Social and Epidemiological Factors in Drug Addiction. In : *Rehabilitating the Narcotic Addict.* Fort Worth, Texas : Institute on New Developments in the Rehabilitation of the Narcotic Addict.

Chitnis, S. (1974) *Drug on the College Campus.* Bombay: Tata Institute of Social Sciences.

Chopra, I.C. (1971) Drug Addiction in India, *Indian Journal of Pharmacology,* 3: 43-50.

Chopra, I.C. and Chopra, R.N. (1965) *Drug Addiction with Special Reference to India.* New Delhi: Council of Scientific and Industrial Research.

Chopra, R.N. and Chopra, G.C. (1935) The present position of Hemp drug addiction in India. *Indian Journal of Medical Research,* 31: 119.

Chopra, R.N. (1940) The Problem of Drug Addiction in India, *Indian Medical Gazetteer,* 75, 556.

——— **(1942)** *Cannabis sativa* in Relation to Mental Diseases and Crime in India. *Indian Journal of Medical Research,* 30: 155-171.

Clausen, John A. (1957) Social Patterns, Personality, and adolescent drug use. In Alexander H. Leighton et al., (eds.), *Explorations in Social Psychiatry*, pp. 232-272. New York: Basic Books.

Cloward, R.A. and Ohlin, L.E. (1960) *Delinquency and Opportunity: A Theory of Delinquent Gangs.* Glencoe, Illinois : Free Press.

Cohen, S. (1971) Profiles of Drug Abusers. In : Pradhan, S.N. (Ed.), *Drug Abuse.* St. Louis, Missouri : C.V. Mosby.

Coleman, J.C. (1982) *Abnormal Psychology and Modern Life.* Bombay: D.B. Taraporevala Sons & Co. (Eighth Indian Reprint).

Connor, Ralph G. (1962) The Self-concepts of Alcoholics. in David J. Pittman and Charles R. Snyder (eds), *Society, Culture, and Drinking Patterns,* pp., 455-67. New York and London : Wiley.

Craig, R.J. (1979) Personality Characteristics of heroin addicts : A review of the empirical imperative with critique. *International Journal of Addiction,* 14: 513-517.

Crowley, T.J. (1972) The Reinforcers for Drug Abuse : Why People Take Drugs. *Comprehensive Psychiatry,* Vol. 13: 51-62.

Dayal, J. (1972) Drug Abuse and Youth. Interdisciplinary Seminar, Directorate of Social Welfare Administration, Delhi Administration, Delhi.

Deb, P.C. and Jindal, R.B. (1974) Drinking in Rural Area— A Study in Selected Villages of Punjab, *Monograph,* Punjab Agricultural University, Ludhiana.

Denton, Jane E. and Beecher, Henry K., (1949) New Analgesics. *Journal of the American Medical Association,* 141 : 1051-1057; 1146-1153.

Dhillon, P.K. and Pawah, P. (1981) A Study of the relationship between drug use, abstract intelligence and feelings of security in the college population of Delhi. In D. Mohan, H.S. Sethi, E. Tongue (eds.), *Current Research in Drug Abuse in India:* 141-148, New Delhi.

Dole, V.P. and Nyswander, M.E. (1967) Rehabilitation of the Street Addict. *Archives of Environmental Health,* Vol. 14: 477-480.

Dube, K.C. (1972) Drug Abuse in Northern India— Observations Concerning Delhi-Agra Region. *Bulletin on Narcotics,* Vol. 1: 49-53.

———, (1977) Prevalence of Drug Abuse in Medical Students. *Bulletin on Narcotics,* 29: 47.

Dube, K.C. and Handa, S.K. (1969) Drug Use in Health and Mental Disorder. *Indian Journal of Psychiatry,* 11: 23-29.

———, **(1971)** Drug Use in Health and Mental Illness in Indian Population. *British Journal of Psychiatry,* 118: 345-346.

Dube, K.C., Kumar, A., Kumar, N. and Gupta, S.P. (1977) Drug Abuse Among College Students— An Interim Report. *Bulletin on Narcotics,* 29(1): 47-61.

Dupont, R.L. (1975) Cited in Return of the Hard Drug Menace. *U.S. News & World Report,* 78(26): 29.

Edwards, A.L. (1971) *Experimental Design in Psychological Research* (3rd Ed.) Holt Rinehart & Winston Inc., Indian edition.

Elkes, Joel J. (1961) Psychotropic Drugs : Observations on Current Views and Future Problems, pp., 65-114 in Conference on Experimental Psychiatry, Western Psychiatric Institute and Clinic, 1959, Lectures on Experimental Psychiatry. Uni. of Pittsburgh Press.

Elnagar, M.N., Maitra, P. and Rao, M.N. (1971) Mental Health in an Indian Rural Community, *British Journal of Psychiatry,* 118: 499.

Field, Peter B. (1962) A New Cross-Cultural study of Drunkenness. In David J. Pittman and Charles R. Snyder (eds.), *Society, Culture, and Drinking Patterns,* pp., 48-74. New York and London : Wiley.

Fisher, R.A. (1950) *Statistical Method for Research Workers,* 11th edn. Edinburg: Oliver & Boyd.

Fort, J.P. (1954) Heroin Addiction among Youngmen. *Psychiatry,* Vol. 17: 251-259.

Frye, R.V. (1980) The Sociobiological Paradigm : A New Approach to Drug Using Behaviour. *Journal of Psychedilic Drugs.* Vol. 12 (1).

Gautam, S., Lodha, R., and Mehta, M. (1991) Personality factors related to drug dependence. Paper presented at 43rd Annual Conference. *Indian Psychiatric Society,* Calicut, Jan., 4-7.

Geller, G.Levine, D.M., and Mamon, J.A.(1989) Knowledge, attitudes, and reported practices of medical students and house staff regarding the diagnosis and treatment of alcoholism. *Journal of Medical Association,* 261: 3115-3120.

Gersick, K.E., Grady, K., Sexton, E., and Lyons, M. (1981) Personality and Sociodemographic Factors in Adolescent Drug Use, *NIDA Research Monograph,* 38 : 39-56.

Goldstein, A., et al. (1974) Researchers isolate opiate receptor. *Behaviour Today* (March) 5 (9), 1.

Greaves, G. (1974) Towards an Existential Theory of Drug Dependence. *Journal of Nervous and Mental Diseases,* Vol. 159 (4): 263-274.

Greene, M.H., and Dupont, R.L. (1974) Heroin Addiction Trends. *American Journal of Psychiatry,* 131(5): 545-50.

Government of India (1977) *Drug Abuse in India.* New Delhi : Ministry of Health and Family Welfare.

Grover, E. (1939) *Psychoanalysis.* London: Staples Press.

Gupta, R., Narang, R.L., Gupta, K.R. and Singh, S. (1986) Drug Abuse among Rickshaw Pullers in Industrial .Town of Ludhiana. *Indian Journal of Psychiatry,* Vol. 28(2): 145-149.

Gupta, S. (1994) Drug abuse on rise. *Tribune,* 5.

Heaton, R.K., and Victor, R.G. (1976) Personality characteristics associated with psychedelic flashbacks in natural and experimental settings. *Journal of Abnormal Psychology,* 85: 83-90.

Heitung, OddG. (1985) The Course of Drug Dependence Related to a Theory of Guilt Awareness and Guilt Feeling, (Gaustad Sykehus, Oslo, Norway). *Journal of Drug Issues,* (Summer), 15, 357-366.

Hendiri, H. and Hass, A. (1985) The Adaptive Significance of Chronic Marijuana Use for Adolescents and Adults. *Advances in Alcohol & Substance Abuse,* 4: 99-115.

Hill, H.E. (1962) The Social Deviant and Initial Addiction to Narcotics and Alcohol. *Quarterly Journal of Studies on Alcohol,* 23: 562-582.

Hill, Harris E.; Haertzen, Charles A.; and Davis, Howard (1962) An MMPI Factor Analytic Study of Alcoholics, Narcotic Addicts and Criminals. *Quarterly Journal of Studies on Alcohol,* 23 : 411-431.

Hill, Harris E.; Haertzen, Charles A.; and Graser, Robert (1960) Personality Characteristics of Narcotic Addicts as Indicated by the MMPI. *Journal of General Psychology,* 62 : 127-139.

Hollingworth, H.L. (1912) The Influence of Caffeine on Mental and Motor Efficiency. *Archives of Psychology,* No. 22.

Hordern, Anthony; Hamilton, Max (1963) Drugs and Moral Treatment. *British Journal of Psychiatry,* 109: 500-509.

Horten, Donald (1943) The Function of Alcohol in Primitive Societies: A Cross-Cultural Study. *Quarterly Journal of Studies on Alcohol,* 4 : 199-320.

Horten, F.W. (1943) On the Question of Pre-existing Personality Difference Between Users and Non-users of Drugs. *Journal of Psychology, 92:* 62-69.

Huba, G.J., and Bentler, P.M. (1982) A Developmental theory of drug Use : Derivation and assessment of a causal modelling approach. In P.B. Baltes & O.G. Brim, Jr. (eds.), *Life Span Development and Behaviour,* Vol. 4, pp. 147-203. New York : Academic Press.

Hunt, G. Halsey; and Odoroff, Maurice E. (1962) Follow up Study of Narcotic Drug Addicts After Hospitalization. U.S. Public Health Service, Public Health Reports, 77: 41-54.

Indian Council of Medical Research (1977) Drug Addiction : An Overview, *ICMR Bulletin,* 7(2)1.

Irwin, T. (1968) Attacking Alcohol as a Disease. *Today's Health,* 46: 21-23.

Jaffe, J.H. (1985) Drug Addiction and Drug Abuse. In Gilman, A.G., Goodman, L.S., Rall, T.W., Murad, F.(eds.), *The Pharmacological Basis of Therapeutics,* pp 532-581. McMillan Publishing Company, (7th ed.).

——— **(1991)** Drug Addiction and Drug Abuse. In Gilman, A.G.; Rall, T.W. and Nies, A.S. (eds.), *Pharmacological Basis of Therapeutics,* pp 522-573. Pergamon Press, 8th Edition.

Jarvik, M.E. (1967) The Psychopharmacological Revolution. *Psych. Today,* 1(1), 51-58.

Jellinek, Elvin M. (1960) The diseage concept of Alcoholism. New Haven : Hillhouse.

Jellinek, Elvin M. and Mc Farland, Ross A. (1940) Analysis of Psychological Experiments on the Effects of Alcohol. *Quarterly Journal of Studies on Alcohol,* 23 : 52-93.

Jessor, Richard et al. (1963) Tri-ethnic Research Project. Research Report No. 25. Unpublished manuscript, Uni. of Colorada.

Jiloha, R.C. & Manjal, G.C. (1985) Adolescent Heroin Smokers of Delhi. *Child Psychiatry Quarterly,* 18, 4.

Jiloha, R.C., and Sahay, M. (1986) Changing trends of drug abuse in Delhi (India) : Experience from a De-Addiction Clinic. *Journal of Personality and Clinical Studies,* 2: 135-140.

Jiloha, R.C. (1990) Nine Years' Profile of a De-addiction Clinic. *Disabilities and Impairments,* 3(2): 133-141.

Jonas, D.F. & Jonas, A.D. (1977) A Bio-anthropologial Overview of Addiction, *Perspectives in Biology and Medicine* (Spring) 345-354.

Keller, Mark (1962) The definition of Alcoholism and the Estimation of its Prevalence. In David J. Pittman and Charles R. Snyder (eds.), *Society, Culture, and Drinking Patterns,* pp. 310-329, New York : Wiley.

Khan, M.Z. (1985) *Drug Abuse among College Youth,* Bombay : Somaiya.

——— **(1989)** A Note on the Nature and Prevalence of Drug Abuse in India. Paper presented at the National Seminar on the Role of Education in the Prevention of Drug Abuse, held at Miranda House, Delhi University, from February 16-18.

Khan, M.Z. and Krishma, K.P. (1984) Research on Drug Dependence in India. *Bulletin on Narcotics,* 34(2): 29-50.

Klausner, Samuel Z. (1964) Sacred and Profane Meanings of Blood and Alcohol. *Journal of Social Psychology,* 64 : 27-43.

Klerman, Gerald L. (1961) Historical Baselines for the Evaluation of Maintenance Drug Therapy of Discharged Psychiatric Patients. In Milton Greenblatt, David T, Levinson, and Gerald L, Klerman (eds.), *Mental Patients in Transition,* pp. 287-301. Spring field, Ill : Thomas.

Knight, R.C. and Praut, C.T. (1951) A Study of Results in Hospital Treatment of Drug-Addicts. *American Journal of Psychiatry,* 108: 303-308.

Kornetsky, Conan (1954) Effects of Anxiety and Morphine on the Anticipation and Perception of Painful Radiant Thermal Stimuli. *Journal of Comparative and Physiological Psychology.* 47 : 130-132.

Kramer, J.F. and Cameron, D.C. (1975) *A Manual on Drug Dependence,* Geneva : World Health Organization (WHO).

Kumar, M.S. (1994) Drugs, AIDS Raise Spectre of Death, *The Hindustan Times,* New Delhi, Vol. LXX, No. 207.

Lewin, Louis (1924) 1931, *Phantastica : Narcotic and Stimulating Drugs : Their use and abuse.* New York : Dutton; London : Routledge. (First published in German) Reissued as *Drugs : Their Use and Abuse* in 1938.

Lettieri, D.J. (1978) Theories of Drug Abuse. In Lettieri, D.J. (ed.) *Drugs and Suicide.* Beverly Hills, California: Sage Publications.

Lindersmith, A.R. (1947) A Sociological Theory of Drug Addiction. *American Journal of Sociology,* Vol. 43: 593-613.

Lindquist, E.F. (1956) *Design and Analysis of Experiment in Psychology and Education.* Boston: Houghton Mifflin Co.

Lisansky, E.S. (1960) The Etiology of Alcoholism : The Role of Psychological Predisposition. *Quarterly Journal of Studies on Alcohol,* 21: 314-343.

———— **(1964)** The Psychological Effects of Alcohol. In Raymond G. McCarthy (ed.), *Alcohol Education for Classroom and Community,* pp 104-121. New York : McGraw-Hill.

Martin, W.R., Hewett, B.B. Baker, A.J., and Haertzen, C.A.(1977) Aspects of the psychopathology and pathophysiology of addiction. *Drug and Alcohol Dependence,* 2: 185-202.

McClelland, D.C., Davis, W.N., Kalin, R. and Wanner, E. (1972) *The Drinking Man.* New York: The Free Press.

McDavid, J.W. and Harari, H. (1968) *Social Psychology.* New York: Harper & Row.

Merton, R.K. (1957) *Social Theory and Social Structure.* Glencoe, Illinois : Free Press.

Milkman, H. and Frosch, W.A. (1973) On the Preferential Abuse of Heroin and Amphetamine. *Journal of Nervous and Mental Diseases,* Vol. 156: 242-48.

Mohan, D. (1976) A Pilot Survey to Determine the Prevalence of Drug Abuse and its Psycho-social Correlation amongst Delhi University Students, Report of Research (Mimeographed), Deptt. of Psychiatry, AIIMS, New Delhi.

Mohan, D. and Arora, A. (1976) Prevalence and Pattern of Drug Abuse among Delhi University College Students. *Journal of Indian Medical Association,* 66, 28.

Mohan, D., Darshan, S. and Neki, J.S. (1977) A Study of Drug Abuse in Rural Areas of Punjab. A preliminary report submitted to the Ministry of Social Welfare, Govt. of India.

Mohan, D., Sharma, A.K. and Sundram, K.R. (1979) Pattern and Prevalence of Opium Use in Rural Punjab. *Bulletin on Narcotics* 1, 31(2), 45.

Mohan, D., Sundram, K.R., Pal, M. and Chawla, P.L. (1981) Drug Abuse Among School Children in Delhi, In Mohan, D. et al. (eds.), *Current Research in Drug Abuse in India.* Delhi: Gemini Printers.

Mohan, D.; Thomas, M.G., and Prabhu, G.G. (1978) Prevalence of drug abuse in a high school population. *Indian Journal of Psychiatry,* 20: 20-26.

Mohsin, S.M. (1984) *Research Methods in Behavioural Sciences,* Orient Longman Ltd.

Nagaraja, J. (1985) Drug addiction among students. *The Tribune,* Nov., 27.

Najam, Najma. (1997) Drug Addiction : Are Political and legal Solutions Effective? *Journal of the Indian Academy of Applied Psychology.* Vol. 23, No. 1-2: 89-94.

Nurco, D.N. Hanlon, T.E., and Shaffer, J.W. (1988) Difference among treatment clinic types in attitude towards narcotic addiction. *Journal of Nervous and Mental Diseases,* 176: 714-718.

Panchanathan, M. and Shanmugaganesan, V. (1992) The Effect of Psychological Stress on Academic Achievement. *Journal of Community Guidance and Research,* Vol. 9 (2): 139-149.

Park, J.E. and Park, K. (1985) *Textbook of Preventive and Social Medicine.* Jabalpur : M/s Banarsidas Bharot.

Parameshran, E.H., and Rao, T.N. (1983) Drug abuse among College students in the twin cities of Hyderabad-Secunderabad. *Social Defence,* 18: 34-36.

Park, Peter (1962) Problem Drinking and Role Deviation : A Study in Incipient Alcoholism. In David J. Pittman and Charles R. Snyder (eds.), *Society, Culture, and Drinking Pattern,* pp. 431-454. New York and London : Wiley.

Paschke, W.R. (1970) The Addiction Cycle : A Learning Theory—Peer Group Model. *Corrective Psychiatry and Journal of Social Therapy,* Vol, 16: 74-81.

Paton, A. (1989) Alcohol Misuse and the hospital doctor. *British Journal of Hospital Medicine,* 42: 394-400.

Pert, C.B., and Synder, S.H. (1973) Opiate receptor : demonstration in nervous tissue. *Science,* 9, 179(4077): 1011-1014.

Pliner, P.L. and Cappell, H.D. (1974) Modification of affective consequences of alcohol : A comparison of social solitary drinking. *Journal of Abnormal Psychology,* 83(4): 418-425.

Poffenberger, Albert T. (1942) *Principles of Applied Psychology.* New York : Appleton.

Ponundurai, R.O., Somasundram, O., Indira, T.P. and Gunashekar, P. (1984) Alcohol and Drug Abuse among Interns. *Indian Journal of Psychiatry,* 26(2): 128-132.

Prasad, M.S. and Thakur, G.P. (1977) *Self - Esteem Inventory.* Agra: Agra Psychological Research Cell.

Rado, S. (1933) The Psychoanalysis of Pharmacothymia : Drug Addiction. *Psycho-analysis Quarterly,* 2: 1-23.

Ram Kumar, V. (1971) Self Concept and Achievement of Forward and Backward Community Students. *Education & Psychology,* 11: 40-46.

Rao, T.S.S., and Kuruvilla, K. (1992) A Study on the copying behaviours of wives of alcoholics. *Indian Journal of Psychiatry,* 34: 359-365.

Rao, D. L. N. M.(1962) Drug Addiction in India. *Journal of Indian Medical Association,* 39, p. 151.

Ray, Oakley, S. (1972) *Drugs, Society and Human Behaviour.* Saint Louis: The C.V. Mosby Company.

Rinkel, M. (1966) Psychedelic Drugs. *American Journal of Psychiatry,* 122(6): 1415-16.

Rosen, A.C. (1960) A Comparative Study of Alcoholic and Psychiatric Patients with the MMPI. *Quarterly Journal of Studies on Alcohol,* 21: 253-266.

Runkel, P.J. and McGrath, J.E. (1972) Research in Human Behaviour. New York: Holt, Rinehart & Winston Inc.

Salmon, R. & Salmon. S.(1977) The Cause of Heroin Addiction : A Review of the Literature. *International Journal of Addictions,* 12: 676-96.

Sargent, S.S. (1948) Reaction to Frustration— A Critique and Hypothesis. *Psychological Review,* 55: 108-114.

Savitt, R.A. (1963) Psychoanalytic Studies on Addiction. *Psychoanalytic Quarterly,* Vol. 32: 43-57.

Saxena, S. and Mohan, D. (1984) Rapid Increase of Heroin Dependence in Delhi: Some Initial Observations. *Indian Journal of Psychiatry,* 26: 41-45.

Schaumann, O. (1954) Analgetica and Protectives System. *Deutsche medizinische Wochenschrift,* 79 : 1571-1573.

Schur, Edwin M. (1962) *Narcotic Addiction in Britain and America : The impact of public policy.* Bloomington : Indiana Uni. Press.

Seldin, N. (1972) The Family of the Addict : A Review of the Literature. *International Journal of the Addictions,* 7(1): 97-107.

Seley, H. (1956) *The Stress of Life.* New York : McGraw-Hill.

Sen, A.K. (1996) Drug Abuse and Psychological Characteristics of the Abusers. In M.C. Paul (ed.), *Drugs, Youth and Society.* New Delhi : Madhu Deep Publishers.

Sethi, B.B. and Manchanda, R. (1977) Drug Abuse among Medical Students, *Indian Journal of Psychiatry,* 19(4): 31-35.

Sethi, B.B. and Trivedi, J.K. (1979) Drug Abuse in a Rural Population. *Indian Journal of Psychiatry,* 21(3): 211.

Sethi, B.B. & Trivedi, J.K. (1979) Drug Abuse in Rural Population. *Indian Journal of Psychiatry,* 21: 2-11.

Shanmugham, T.E. (1978) A Study of drug abuse among college students. Unpublished Project sponsored by the Deptt. of Social Welfare, Government of India.

————, (1981) Personality factors underlying drug abuse among college students. In D. Mohan, H.S. Sethi; E. Tongue (eds.), *Current Research in Drug Abuse in India.* pp. 44-48. New Delhi.

Singh, A. and Singh, S. (1980) Drug Abuse Amongst Students in Punjab. *Indian Psychological Review,* 19, 4: 1-7.

Singh, D.R. and Khan, M.Z. (1981) Sub-cultural Aspects of Drug Use in an Indian University, In Mohan, D. et al.(eds.), *Current Research Drug Abuse in India,* pp 119-131. Delhi: Gemini Printers.

Singh, S. (1977) A Comparative Study of Personality Characteristics of Drug Abuse Among University Students. Ph.D. thesis submitted to University of Delhi (Unpublished).

Singh, G. (1978) Alcohol Consumption in Punjab. *Indian Journal of Psychiatry,* Vol. 20: 212-16.

———— (1979) Drug Abuse among Medical Students (I) Prevalence and Pattern of Use. *Indian Journal of Psychiatry,* 31(4), 332.

———— (1979) Drug Use Among Medical Students (II) Socio-demographic and Personality Factors. *Indian Journal of Psychiatry,* 21: 339-44.

Singh, G. and Lal, B. (1978) Alcohol Consumption in Punjab, paper presented at 30th Annual Conference of Indian Psychiatric Society. New Delhi.

Singh, H. (1975) Drug Abuse Control, Editorial. *Social Defence,* Vol. X, No. 40.

Singh, S. (1978) A Comparative Study of Personality Characteristics of Drug users among University Students, Ph.D. thesis submitted to University of Delhi (Unpublished), 1977.

Singh, G. and Lal, B. (1977) Drug Abuse in Punjab. Data furnished to the Committee on drug addiction.

———— (1978) Drug abuse in Punjab. *British Journal of Addiction.*

Smart, R.G. Murray, G.F. and Arif, A. (1988). Drug abuse and prevention programmes in 29 Countries. *International Journal of the Addictions,* 23: 1-17.

Snyder, Charles R. (1964) Inebriety, Alcoholism, and Anomie. In Marshall E. Clinard (ed.), *Anomie and Deviant Behaviour : A Discussion and Critique,* pp. 189-212. New York : Free Press.

Sonnedecker, Glenn (1963) Emergence and concept of the problem of addiction, pp. 14-22 in symposium on the History of Narcotic Drug Addiction Problems : Proceedings. Edited by Robert B. Livingston. U.S. Public Health Service, Publication No. 1050. Washington, Government Printing Office - A brief historical overview.

Spencer, C., and Navaratnam, V. (1980) Social background and attitudes towards drugs as predictors of drug use among Malaysian students. *Drug and Alcohol Dependence,* 5: 411-419.

Steffenhagen, R.A. (1974) Drug Abuse and Related Phenomena: An Adlerian Approach. *Journal of Individual Psychology,* Vol. 30: 238-250.

Stone, Gregory P. (1962) Drinking styles and Status Arrangements. In David J. Pittman and Charles R. Snyder (eds.), *Society, Culture, and Drinking Patterns,* pp. 121-140. New York and London : Wiley.

Sutherland, E.H., Schroeder, H.G., and Tordella, C.L. (1950) Personality Traits and the Alcoholic : A Critique of Existing Studies. *Quarterly Journal of Studies on Alcohol,* 11: 547-561.

Syme, L. (1957) Personality Characteristics and the Alcoholic. *Quarterly Journal of Studies on Alcohol,* 18: 288-302.

Thacore, V.R. (1972) Drug Abuse in India with Special Reference to Lucknow. *Indian Journal of Psychiatry,* 14: 247-61.

United States Reports (1986) Current Agency Roles in Drug Enforcement, Policy and Reducing Drug Demand. Americas habit. Drug Abuse, Drug Trafficking and Organized Crime. President's Commission on Organized Crime Report to the President and the Attorney General, U.S.A.

Varma, V.K., and Dang, R. (1978) A Study of attitudes, perception, and exposure to drug use and its relation to socio-demographic variables. *Indian Journal of Psychiatry,* 20: 318-323.

Varma, V.K. and Dang, R. (1979) Non-Medical use of Drugs among School and College Students. *Indian Journal of Psychiatry,* 21: 228-34.

Varma, V.K., Ghosh, A., Singh, S. and Wig, N.N. (1977) Drug Abuse among College Students. *Indian Journal of Psychiatry,* 19(1), 1-10.

Varma, V.K., Singh, A., Singh, S.; Malhotra, A. (1980) Extent and Pattern of Alcohol Use and Alcohol Related Problems in North India. *Indian Journal of Psychiatry,* 22(4): 331-337.

Veeraraghavan, V. (1972) *Students and Drug Use.* New Delhi: Rachna Publishers.

———— **(1980)** Drug Abuse among University Students. Paper presented at the National and Regional Conference on Drug Abuse, New Delhi.

Venkoba Rao, A., Chinnian, R.R., Pradeep, D. and Rajgopal, P. (1975) Cannabis *(Ganja)* and Cognition. *Indian Journal of Psychiatry,* 17: 233.

Weech, A.A. (1966) The Narcotic Addict and the Street. *Archives of General Psychiatry,* Vol. 14: 299-306.

Weil, A. (1972) *The Natural Mind.* Boston : Houghton Mifflin.

————**, (1973)** Dynamics of Drug Dependence. Implications of Conditioning Theory for Research and Treatment. *Archives of General Psychiatry,* Vol. 28: 611-16.

Wilson, J. Q. (1975) The Return of Heroin. *Commentary,* 49(4): 46-50.

Westermeyer, J. (1971) Use of Alcohol and Opium by the Meo of Lao. *American Journal of Psychiatry,* 127(8): 1019-1023.

Wikler, Abraham. (1952) A Psychodynamic Study of a Patient During Experimental Self regulated Readdiction to Morphine. *Psychiatric Quarterly,* 26 : 270-293.

Wikler, A. (1962) Psychological bases of drug abuse. In proceedings of White House Conference (1962) Washington D.C. : Government Printing Office.

————**, (1962)** Drug Addiction Vol. 8. In Frederick Tice (Editor) *Practice of Medicine,* pp. 17-58. Hagerstown: Mds Prior.

Wikler, A.; and Rasor, Robert W. (1953) Psychiatric aspects of drug addiction. *American Journal of Medicine,* 14 : 566-570.

World Health Organization, Expert Committee on Alcohol (1954) First Report. World Health Organisation, Technical Report Series, 1954, No. 84.

Zubin, Joseph; and Katz, Martin M. (1964) Psychopharmacology and Personality, pp. 367-395 in Symposium on Personality Change, University of Texas, *Personality Change.* Edited by Philip Worchel and Donn Byrne. New York : Wiley.

Zwerling, Israel; and Rosenbaum, Milton (1959) Alcoholic Addiction and Personality (Nonpsychotic conditions). Vol. 1, pages 623-644 in *American Handbook of Psychiatry.* Edited by Silvano Arieti. New York : Basic Books.

Zoja, Luigi (1984) Sucht Als Unbewusster Versuch Zur Initiation. Teil 1. *Addiction as an Unconscious Attempts Towards Initiation:* ***1 (German)*** *Analytische Psychologic.* Vol. 15: 110-125.

INDEX